what color is your parachute?
for teens

WHAT COLOR IS YOUR PARACHUTE?
FOR TEENS

Discovering Yourself, Defining Your Future

RICHARD NELSON BOLLES and **CAROL CHRISTEN**

with Jean M. Blomquist

TEN SPEED PRESS

Berkeley | Toronto

Ten Speed Press
Box 7123
Berkeley, California 94707
www.tenspeed.com

Distributed in Australia by Simon and Schuster Australia, in Canada by Ten Speed Press Canada, in New Zealand by Southern Publishers Group, in South Africa by Real Books, and in the United Kingdom and Europe by Publishers Group UK.

Cover and text design by Betsy Stromberg
Illustration on pages 70–71 by Ann Miya

Library of Congress Cataloging-in-Publication Data

Bolles, Richard Nelson.
  What color is your parachute? for teens : discovering yourself, defining your future / Richard Nelson Bolles and Carol Christen, with Jean M. Blomquist.
      p. cm.
  Includes bibliographical references and index.
  ISBN-13: 978-1-58008-713-1 (alk. paper)
  ISBN-10: 1-58008-713-2 (alk. paper)
   1. Teenagers--Vocational guidance. 2. Job hunting. I. Christen, Carol.
II. Blomquist, Jean M. III. Title.
  HF5381.B63513 2006
  331.702083'5--dc22
                            2006005029

Printed in the USA

  5 6 7 8 9 10 — 10 09 08 07

My Parachute

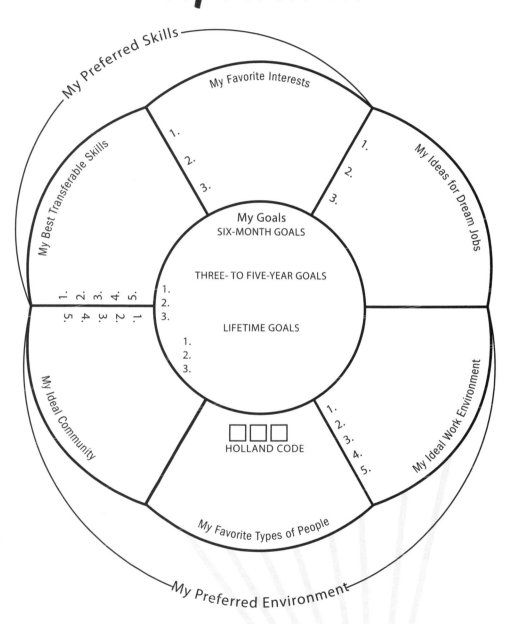

My Preferred Skills

My Favorite Interests
1.
2.
3.

My Best Transferable Skills

My Ideas for Dream Jobs
1.
2.
3.

My Goals
SIX-MONTH GOALS

THREE- TO FIVE-YEAR GOALS
1.
2.
3.

LIFETIME GOALS
1.
2.
3.

1.
2.
3.
4.
5.

1.
2.
3.
4.
5.

HOLLAND CODE

My Ideal Community

My Ideal Work Environment
1.
2.
3.
4.
5.

My Favorite Types of People

My Preferred Environment

To make this form easier
to use, photocopy this page
and enlarge it.

Contents

PART ONE

discovering your dream job

PART TWO

on the way to your future

PART THREE

landing your dream job...and more

Acknowledgments

BOUQUETS OF THANKS TO ALL WHO HELPED WITH THIS BOOK, ESPECIALLY THE FOLLOWING:

Phil Wood, for calling to ask about my interest in adapting *Parachute* for teens. Richard N. Bolles, for writing the original *What Color Is Your Parachute?* and enabling millions of people—myself included—to find jobs and careers they love. Winifred Wood, for issuing the challenge that planted the seeds for this book. Lily Binns, my wise-beyond-her-years and highly competent editor at Ten Speed Press. The entire team at Ten Speed Press who designs, produces, publicizes, markets, sells, and ships this book. Colleagues Sue Cullen, Rich Feller, Letta Hlavachek, Jim Kell, Brian McIvor, Marty Nemko, and Daniel Porot for giving me helpful suggestions and access to their brilliant minds. David Maxwell, chair of the Business Department at Ernest Righetti High School; Jeff Stein and Matt Aydelott of the workforce development projects at Cuesta College; and Professor Jim Howland of the Technical/Professional Writing Program at Cal Poly, San Luis Obispo, for allowing me access to their students. The hundreds of teens and young adults who shared their lessons, hopes, and fears. Cynthia Campbell, for being such a caring friend and psychic about when to call. Muriel Christen-Jones, my mother, for her unconditional support of this project, and me. Serena Brewer, my daughter, for her encouragement *(Leap... and the net will appear)*, brainstorming, giving me access to her world-wide network, and, most importantly, taking the time to find a career path she loves. And to JCR, my best friend since 1965, for endless cups of tea, grocery shopping, making dinner, and keeping CR Farms going while I was otherwise engaged. Your love is my safety net.

With deep gratitude,
Carol Christen
parachutefirstaid@hotmail.com

Introduction

This book is about you—and your future—which is, of course, a very fascinating subject! We want to explore who you are, what's important to you, and what you like to do. Why? We believe life is meant to be lived to the fullest, and we want you to have just that kind of life. We want to help you discover what you'd love to do with your life, especially work that you will love.

"But I'm only fourteen (or fifteen, sixteen, seventeen, eighteen)," you say. "I'm too young to be thinking about my life's work!"

We think your teen years are a great time to be thinking about your life's work. As a young adult, you're beginning to discover what's important to you—how you like to spend your time, who you like to be with, what classes are interesting (and which ones aren't). And most likely, you're becoming aware that some adults you know—teachers, parents, coaches, and others—really enjoy what they're doing, and others don't. We want to help you find work that you'll enjoy—work that's fun, satisfying, and challenging all rolled into one.

Who Should Read This Book?

This book is for you if any of the following apply to you:

- You care about how you'll earn a living.

- You have career goals but may not know how to reach them.

- You want to find a college major that's right for you.

- You want to take as much control over your life as possible.

- You hope to become financially independent as soon as possible.

- You hope to find a fun job to finance your life while you figure out what you really want to do for work, what kind of a life you want to have (and how you can get that life), and who, as a person, you really want to be.

In short, if you want work that you love and if you're willing to spend some time learning about yourself and about the world of work, this book is for you.

Why Do I Need This Book?

Finding a job you'll love takes not only time and energy but also job-search awareness and skills. Chances are, even if you're quite busy now, you have time and energy you can devote to increasing your awareness of what kind of work is good for you and enjoyable, and to developing skills that will help you find that kind of work. When we talked with young adults engaged in their own job hunt, they often told us that they could have made better use of their time in school if they had known how to use it to make themselves more employable. Richard N. Bolles, one of the authors of this book, has a website (www.JobHuntersBible.com) through which he hears from job hunters around the world. He often receives letters from people who say they were surprised by how hard it was to find a job or how long it took them. We want you to be prepared, not surprised. We want to help you to work smart, which means developing job-search savvy that will help you now and throughout your adult life. If you use your time now to do some planning for how you want to earn a living, you stand a good chance of achieving your career goals. Even if you're not sure what you want to do—and you're not alone there (many adults feel that way too)—we'll help you discover just what kind of job will be a good and satisfying one for you. You'll learn what you need to know about yourself and about the world of work so that you can make good choices about how you want to live and work.

Why Did We Write This Book?

We want you to find work that you love. We want to give you the skills necessary to find out what it is you love to do, and to find a job where you can do just that.

In our work, we meet thousands of adults who don't know how to find work they love. When they were in high school, very few of them learned effective job-search skills—usually because classes in job-search skills weren't even offered. For those planning on college, few received helpful guidance on selecting a major, even though finding the right major can be an important step toward finding a great job. Almost none received guidance in how to discover what they most wanted out of work and life, or what employers wanted and expected of them. We want you to have both the skills and the knowledge necessary to find good and rewarding work throughout your life.

The world of work changes constantly. Some jobs disappear, while new ones appear; others change significantly because of scientific advances, new technology, or the needs and expectations of society. The strength or weakness of the economy also affects the number and types of jobs available. If you have solid job-search skills and know what you really want to do, you can thrive—or, like a cat, always land on your feet—even when the work world changes.

Perhaps you've had a few part-time jobs already. Maybe you liked your work, maybe you didn't. More likely, you liked some parts of your work but not others. Those work experiences—and all your life experiences—are valuable because they can tell you important things about yourself and about the work you want to do.

Are you ready for an adventure? Great! That's what this book can offer you—an adventure in discovering more about you and what's most important to you. So let's get started by looking at your life and discovering your answer to this question: How do I find work I will love?

discovering your dream job

Hold on to those dreams of being a firefighter or ship captain or doctor or nurse. Don't let others tell you that those are silly dreams. I think so many people end up doing, consciously or not, what others expect of them, or they settle for less because they think achieving their dream is too hard.

—ROB SANDERS, PEDIATRIC PHYSICIAN, AGE 28

DO you know what your dream job is? If you're absolutely sure what you long to do, that's great. But maybe you aren't so sure. That's fine too. Perhaps your dream job will become clear over time, as it does for many people. Whichever is true for you, we believe that the search for your dream job is very important. Because so much of your adult life will be spent working, finding work you love will help make your whole life more satisfying, gratifying, and fun.

Speaking of fun, that's what the process of finding your dream job can be. You'll become a detective looking for clues in your own life, discovering what matters most to you: what you love to do, who your favorite types of people are, and where you'd like to do what you love to do. As you gather together these clues from your own life, you'll discover the foundation for finding work you love.

Most people don't find their dream job because they think that having their whole dream come true isn't possible. They may pursue just part of it—whatever they think might come true. The problem is, if you only pursue half your dream, your whole heart won't be in it. You'll pursue that half dream halfheartedly, and half your dream is all that will ever come true.

We want you to discover and pursue your whole dream with your whole heart! To do this, we'll begin by asking you three basic questions in part 1 of this book: What do you like to do and what are you good at? Who (that is, what kind of people) do you like to do those things with? Where do you like to do those things? Once you know your *what*, *who*, and *where*, you'll be ready to explore how to find work you'll love. We'll look at the question *how* in part 3. But before we explore how, in part 2 we'll look at some things you can do right now to get yourself on your way to your dream job.

Before you begin your detective work, though, you may have one other question you'd like answered: Why is this book called *What Color Is Your Parachute? for Teens*. The "for teens" part is clear—it means this book is for you. But what about this "parachute" thing? We use the image of a parachute, made of yards and yards of billowing, multicolored fabric, because a parachute helps you land where you want and need to land. In the case of finding your dream job, your parachute is made up of all your skills, goals, and desires or dreams. Everyone's parachute is a different color because every person's skills, goals, and desires come together in a different way. As you explore the questions *what, who,* and *where* (and *how* in part 3), you'll list your most important discoveries about yourself on your own parachute (see My Parachute, p. v).

You may want to keep your answers in a journal and return to these questions after a few months, after your first job, or after you get some technical training or go on to college. Your answers will grow as you grow and as you accumulate more life and work experience. The answers to some questions may not be very clear now, but they'll become clearer over time. And answers that you're certain of now may remain steady through the years, which will confirm their importance in your life.

When you put all your *what, who,* and *where* clues in one place (on your parachute), you'll have a clear and concise picture to guide you in finding work you'll love. You'll know what color your unique parachute is. Whatever color it is, your parachute will be beautiful and strong, and it will help you land in just the right spot in life—in a job you'll love.

what you love to do

YOUR FAVORITE INTERESTS

AND BEST SKILLS

Why does this first chapter focus on what you love to do? Because what you love to do reveals your interests and your skills. Those favorite interests and skills, especially the skills that you most enjoy using (which we call your "best" skills), are major clues to finding work that you'll love. Let's look at your interests first.

Discover Your Favorite Interests

Take a moment and think about how you spend your time. Of the things that you do, what is the most fun? What captures your attention—and your imagination? What is your favorite subject in school? Everyone will have different answers—his or her unique combination of interests. Diane, for example, loves movies. Jeff spends hours on his computer, trying to figure out new ways of doing things. Jessica loves plants and gardening, and Dean lives and breathes sports—all kinds of sports. So how might these different interests lead Diane, Jeff, Jessica, and Dean to work they'll love?

Let's take a look at Diane's interests first. She loves movies. If she chooses movies (or filmmaking) as a career field, what could she do? Our first thoughts usually go to the obvious: she could be an actress, a screen-writer, or a director—or maybe a movie critic (then she'd get to see lots of movies). But Diane has many more possibilities to choose from. She could be a researcher (especially for historical movies), travel expert (to scout locations), interior designer (to design sets), carpenter (to build sets), painter (for backdrops and the like), costume designer, makeup artist, hair stylist, camera operator, lighting technician, sound mixer or editor, com-poser (for soundtracks), stunt person, caterer, personal assistant (to the director or cast members), first aid person, secretary, publicist, account-ant, or any number of other things.

Diane also loves animals and is really good at training them. She could combine her interests —movies and animals—with her skill in training animals, and become an animal trainer (or "wrangler" as they're some-times called) for the film industry. That's a job most people wouldn't think of when considering careers in film.

What kind of career might Jeff's interest in computers lead to? He could be a programmer, do computer repair, or develop video games. Or because he loves art as well as computers, maybe he'll work with Diane in the film industry as a computer graphics designer (for special effects). Jessica, because of her interest in plants and gardening, could become a florist, landscape designer, botanist, or developer of plant hybrids, or she might run her own landscape and lawn maintenance business. Dean's love of sports might lead him to be a professional athlete, a coach, or maybe—because he loves working with kids and has a little brother with cerebral palsy—he might teach adaptive physical education, helping children with physical disabilities get the exercise they need.

As you can see, your interests can lead you in many different directions in your work life. It's true that interests change with time, age, and exposure to new people, places, and experiences. But it's also true that your interests now may be with you all your life, so naming your interests is a great starting place for finding work you'll love. Let's take a closer look at your interests now.

DISCOVERY EXERCISE

How to Find What You Love to Do: Naming Your Interests

Write your answer to each question on a slip of paper or Post-it note.

- When you've got free time, what do you like to do?
- What's your favorite subject in school?
- When you're in the magazine section of your school library or a bookstore, what type of magazine (computer, fashion, sports, and so forth) will you pick up and read first?
- Fill in the blank: When I'm _____, I lose track of time and don't want anyone or anything to disturb me.
- If someone asked you what your favorite interests are, what would you say?

After you've answered all the questions, put your answers in order (your favorite interest first, second favorite next, and so on) and then write your top three interests in the My Favorite Interests section of My Parachute (p. v).

Good work! You're off to a great start.

Skills You Enjoy Using

Your interests are closely tied to your skills, especially the skills that you most enjoy using. We call these your "best" skills because they are your best bet to finding a job that you love. How? It's simple: when you know what your skills are, especially your best skills, you can look for jobs that use those particular skills most frequently—those are the jobs that you most likely will enjoy doing.

"But I don't have any skills," you say.

Chances are you have more skills than you realize. Often our best skills are so close to us that we're not even aware of them. They come so easily and naturally that we think anybody can do them the way we do. It's true that you probably don't have as many skills as your older brother or sister has, and they probably don't have as many skills as your parents or favorite teachers have. Skills grow as we grow—for example, as we gain more life experience, pursue further education, or work at a particular job for an extended period of time. But by the time you're a teenager, you've already developed many skills.

Transferable Skills

At its most basic, a skill is a developed aptitude or ability. A skill can range from a basic life skill like being able to turn on a water faucet (which we can't do till we're tall enough to reach the faucet and strong enough to turn the handle) to a more advanced skill like being able to drive a car. (Skills are also called "talents" or "gifts." In this book, we'll use the word "skills.")

There are many different types of skills, and the most basic are transferable skills. Along with your interests, transferable skills are the foundation for knowing what you love to do. Sometimes they're also called "functional" skills because these are skills you do, such as gathering information or data, or working with people or things. Let's say you like to skateboard. (Skateboarding could be one of the interests you named above.) When you skateboard, you work with some "thing" (a skateboard) and skateboarding is what you do with the skateboard. What are your transferable skills? You have hand-eye-foot coordination, physical agility, and exceptional balance, as well as the ability to make split-second decisions and take risks. Nothing limits these skills to skateboarding. They'd be valuable in (that is, transferable to) work as a surfing instructor, lumberjack, mountain rescue crew member, or any number of other jobs.

Transferable skills can be divided into three different types: physical, mental, and interpersonal. Physical skills primarily use the hands or body and generally involve working with things (such as materials, equipment, or objects, like your skateboard). Working with things includes working with nature (plants and animals). Mental skills primarily use the mind and generally involve working with data/information or ideas. Interpersonal skills primarily involve working with people (or animals!) as you serve or help them with their needs or problems. (We call these different types of skills "Skill TIPs"—that is, skills that work with Things, Information/Ideas,

DISCOVERY EXERCISE

How to Find What You Love to Do: Identifying Your Skills

You begin to identify your skills by looking at your life. Think about projects you have completed, recent problems that you solved, your hobbies, and the activities you do for fun. These can be experiences from school, volunteer work, paid work, or your free time. Select a project or activity you enjoyed that had an outcome—writing a paper, helping to organize an activity, or learning something new, such as a sport or hobby. Write a short paragraph that describes how you completed your project or worked out a solution to the problem you had.

Now give your project, problem, or activity a title. Then answer these questions:

- *Goal or Problem:* What was your goal—that is, what were you trying to accomplish? Or, what was the problem you were trying to solve?
- *Obstacles:* What made achieving your goal (or solving the problem) difficult? How did you overcome these obstacles?
- *Time Frame:* How long did it take you to achieve your goal or solve your problem?
- *Outcome:* What happened? Did things go as you expected, or did something unexpected happen?

or People.) So, if one of your skills is skateboarding, your transferable skills include physical skills (hand-eye-foot coordination, agility, balance, and skateboard maneuvering) and mental skills (split-second decision making). Skateboarding can also involve using interpersonal skills, especially if you enjoy teaching others how to skateboard or do specialized trick and maneuvers.

Why Are My Transferable Skills Important?

Your transferable skills are particularly important as you look for your dream job because they can be transferred from one place to another, to any field or career you choose, regardless of where you first picked them up or how long you've had them. For example, your ability to swim is a skill that can be transferred to, or used in, work as a lifeguard, a swim coach, or a counselor at a summer camp.

Transferable skills are the basic building blocks of any job or career. Most jobs rely on just four to seven main skills. (These groups of skills are sometimes called "skill sets.") That's why it's so important to identify yours. If you know your best transferable skills, you can compare the skills needed in a job with those you do well and enjoy using. That will help you find a job you'll love. The more of your best skills you use in a job, the more likely you will love it.

> **HOW DO TRANSFERABLE SKILLS HELP ME FIND MY DREAM JOB?**
>
> Every job has certain core activities or tasks that you do over and over. To do these activities or tasks, you need to have certain skills. If you know what skills you most enjoy using, you'll be able to compare the skills needed in a job to your own best skills. If a job doesn't use most of your best skills, you won't be happy with it.

Need a little inspiration on what kind of story to write? Serena Brewer was a seventeen-year-old high school senior when she wrote the following story.

MY COMMUNITY SERVICE PROJECT
by Serena Brewer • The Athenian School (Danville, CA)

The high school I attended required seniors to design and complete a community service project. My project stemmed from my love of teaching skiing and a unique opportunity that came from a phone call with my dad.

My dad was a school superintendent for a school district near the mountains. One of his schools offered alpine and cross-country skiing to fourth to eighth graders for P.E. credit. The school had a class for Down syndrome kids. I asked if the kids from this class got to go skiing. When my dad said no, I instantly knew what my community service project would be. Most kids who have this syndrome have enough motor coordination to participate in activities like skiing. I wanted to give these kids a chance to have fun in the snow and maybe even ski.

After overcoming his initial resistance, my dad put me in contact with the woman who taught the class for students with Down syndrome and with a family that might be willing to let me work with their kids. I created an outline of what we would do and how I would teach them. I met with the teacher and the family. I convinced the local ski resort to donate ski rentals and access to the rope tow and beginner's area. It turned out that the kids didn't remember much from one lesson to another. But they did experience something new and had fun.

My high school was one of a group of schools around the world that emphasize community service. The head of my school submitted my project in a competition. I was amazed when I was chosen to receive an international community service award for my project.

COMMUNITY SERVICE PROJECT

Goal or problem: Designing a community service project to meet graduation requirements.
Obstacles: Convincing people that students with Down syndrome could learn to ski and enjoy the snow just like other elementary students; obtaining free ski rentals and ski passes.
Time frame: Three months (January–March)
Outcome: Five Down syndrome students were able to experience skiing; community service award received.

(Incidentally, this young woman decided to become a medical doctor. You can read more about how she uses her skills and interests in the appendix, p. 150.)

Are you ready for a little detective work? Good! Let's turn to your life now and begin to identify your skills and, in particular, your best skills.

Discover Your Skills

Now that you've read My Community Service Project, reread your own story. Using the list of Skill TIPs (pp. 16–18), identify the skills you use in your story. All of the skills in this list are transferable skills—skills that you can use in many different settings or jobs. You may want to photocopy the Skill TIPs list before you begin so you'll have a fresh copy to use if you want to do this exercise in the future or if you want to share it with a friend.

As you go through the Skill TIPs list, put a check mark in box #1 under each skill that you used. For example, if you used the skill "making" in your story (you made a dress or a sculpture), put a check mark in box #1 underneath "making" in Skills with Things (p. 16).

Here are a few of the skills that Serena, who wrote about her community service project, might have selected:

- Skills with Things (physical): motor/physical coordination with my whole body (skiing)

- Skills with Information (mental): imagining, inventing, creating, or designing new ideas (designing a skiing program for students with Down syndrome)

- Skills with People (interpersonal): teaching, training, or designing educational events (teaching skiing to students with Down syndrome and designing the program to teach them to ski)

Now that you've gone through the process and understand how it works, write four more stories so you have a total of five. If you wrote about a project the first time, try writing about something else: teaching your little sister how to ride a bike, learning to ice-skate, dealing with a

> **DISCOVER YOUR SKILLS**
>
> ---
>
> 1. Review your story.
> 2. Identify the skills you used.
> 3. Check your skills off on the Skill TIPs list (pp. 16–18).

Skills with Things

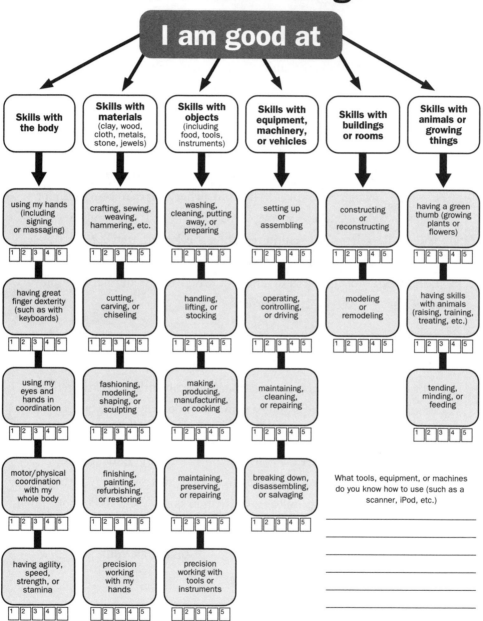

I am good at

Skills with the body	Skills with materials (clay, wood, cloth, metals, stone, jewels)	Skills with objects (including food, tools, instruments)	Skills with equipment, machinery, or vehicles	Skills with buildings or rooms	Skills with animals or growing things
using my hands (including signing or massaging)	crafting, sewing, weaving, hammering, etc.	washing, cleaning, putting away, or preparing	setting up or assembling	constructing or reconstructing	having a green thumb (growing plants or flowers)
1 2 3 4 5	1 2 3 4 5	1 2 3 4 5	1 2 3 4 5	1 2 3 4 5	1 2 3 4 5
having great finger dexterity (such as with keyboards)	cutting, carving, or chiseling	handling, lifting, or stocking	operating, controlling, or driving	modeling or remodeling	having skills with animals (raising, training, treating, etc.)
1 2 3 4 5	1 2 3 4 5	1 2 3 4 5	1 2 3 4 5	1 2 3 4 5	1 2 3 4 5
using my eyes and hands in coordination	fashioning, modeling, shaping, or sculpting	making, producing, manufacturing, or cooking	maintaining, cleaning, or repairing		tending, minding, or feeding
1 2 3 4 5	1 2 3 4 5	1 2 3 4 5	1 2 3 4 5		1 2 3 4 5
motor/physical coordination with my whole body	finishing, painting, refurbishing, or restoring	maintaining, preserving, or repairing	breaking down, disassembling, or salvaging		
1 2 3 4 5	1 2 3 4 5	1 2 3 4 5	1 2 3 4 5		
having agility, speed, strength, or stamina	precision working with my hands	precision working with tools or instruments			
1 2 3 4 5	1 2 3 4 5	1 2 3 4 5			

What tools, equipment, or machines do you know how to use (such as a scanner, iPod, etc.)

_____

_____

_____

_____

_____

_____

Skills with Information

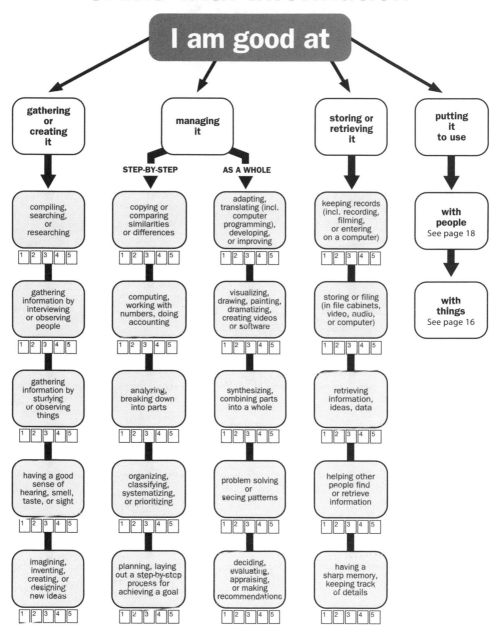

I am good at

gathering or creating it

compiling, searching, or researching

| 1 | 2 | 3 | 4 | 5 |

gathering information by interviewing or observing people

| 1 | 2 | 3 | 4 | 5 |

gathering information by studying or observing things

| 1 | 2 | 3 | 4 | 5 |

having a good sense of hearing, smell, taste, or sight

| 1 | 2 | 3 | 4 | 5 |

imagining, inventing, creating, or designing new ideas

| 1 | 2 | 3 | 4 | 5 |

managing it

STEP-BY-STEP

copying or comparing similarities or differences

| 1 | 2 | 3 | 4 | 5 |

computing, working with numbers, doing accounting

| 1 | 2 | 3 | 4 | 5 |

analyzing, breaking down into parts

| 1 | 2 | 3 | 4 | 5 |

organizing, classifying, systematizing, or prioritizing

| 1 | 2 | 3 | 4 | 5 |

planning, laying out a step-by-step process for achieving a goal

| 1 | 2 | 3 | 4 | 5 |

AS A WHOLE

adapting, translating (incl. computer programming), developing, or improving

| 1 | 2 | 3 | 4 | 5 |

visualizing, drawing, painting, dramatizing, creating videos or software

| 1 | 2 | 3 | 4 | 5 |

synthesizing, combining parts into a whole

| 1 | 2 | 3 | 4 | 5 |

problem solving or seeing patterns

| 1 | 2 | 3 | 4 | 5 |

deciding, evaluating, appraising, or making recommendations

| 1 | 2 | 3 | 4 | 5 |

storing or retrieving it

keeping records (incl. recording, filming, or entering on a computer)

| 1 | 2 | 3 | 4 | 5 |

storing or filing (in file cabinets, video, audio, or computer)

| 1 | 2 | 3 | 4 | 5 |

retrieving information, ideas, data

| 1 | 2 | 3 | 4 | 5 |

helping other people find or retrieve information

| 1 | 2 | 3 | 4 | 5 |

having a sharp memory, keeping track of details

| 1 | 2 | 3 | 4 | 5 |

putting it to use

with people
See page 18

with things
See page 16

Skills with People

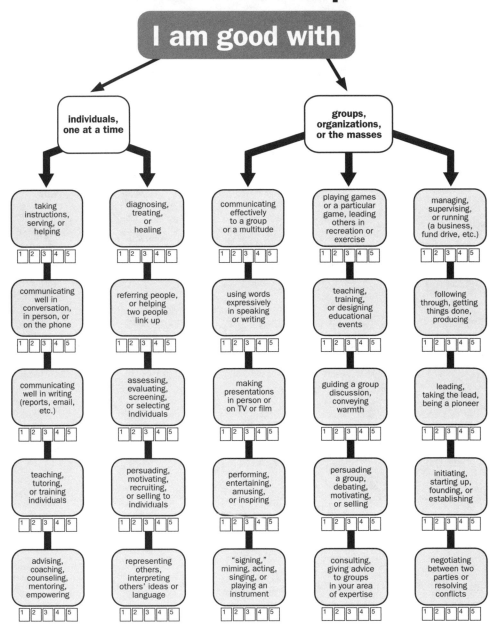

I am good with

individuals, one at a time

groups, organizations, or the masses

taking instructions, serving, or helping
1 2 3 4 5

diagnosing, treating, or healing
1 2 3 4 5

communicating effectively to a group or a multitude
1 2 3 4 5

playing games or a particular game, leading others in recreation or exercise
1 2 3 4 5

managing, supervising, or running (a business, fund drive, etc.)
1 2 3 4 5

communicating well in conversation, in person, or on the phone
1 2 3 4 5

referring people, or helping two people link up
1 2 3 4 5

using words expressively in speaking or writing
1 2 3 4 5

teaching, training, or designing educational events
1 2 3 4 5

following through, getting things done, producing
1 2 3 4 5

communicating well in writing (reports, email, etc.)
1 2 3 4 5

assessing, evaluating, screening, or selecting individuals
1 2 3 4 5

making presentations in person or on TV or film
1 2 3 4 5

guiding a group discussion, conveying warmth
1 2 3 4 5

leading, taking the lead, being a pioneer
1 2 3 4 5

teaching, tutoring, or training individuals
1 2 3 4 5

persuading, motivating, recruiting, or selling to individuals
1 2 3 4 5

performing, entertaining, amusing, or inspiring
1 2 3 4 5

persuading a group, debating, motivating, or selling
1 2 3 4 5

initiating, starting up, founding, or establishing
1 2 3 4 5

advising, coaching, counseling, mentoring, empowering
1 2 3 4 5

representing others, interpreting others' ideas or language
1 2 3 4 5

"signing," miming, acting, singing, or playing an instrument
1 2 3 4 5

consulting, giving advice to groups in your area of expertise
1 2 3 4 5

negotiating between two parties or resolving conflicts
1 2 3 4 5

friend who gossiped about you behind your back. Having five stories will help you find the different kinds of skills you use in different situations. Number each story using numbers 2 through 5. (You've already written story #1.) Next, for story #2, place check marks in box #2 for each skill you used. Do this for each of the remaining stories, #3, #4, and #5. (If you want to brighten up the list and you like to use colored pens, you may want to use a different color for each story.) You may find that in each story, you used many different skills—some in the "thing" category, others in the "idea/information" category, and still others in the "people" category.

Identify Your Best Transferable Skills

Now we're ready to find which skills are your "best" ones—the ones you most enjoy using. Every job will include some tasks or need a few skills you don't much care for. But to find a job you'll enjoy, you want to know which skills you really like to use and which ones you do well. Think about big chunks of time. What skills do you like enough to use over and over all day long?

You have both "can-do" and "want-to" skills. Can-do skills are ones you don't want to use very often. For example, you probably have the skills to wash all the dishes from Thanksgiving dinner for thirty people. But how often would you want to use those skills—all day, every day, once a year, never?

Want-to skills are ones you enjoy using and could do over and over again, several times a day, and not go crazy. It's important to remember that everyone's can-do and want-to skills are different. The world needs people with different skills, people who enjoy using different skills.

Look at your list and see which skills are can-do and which are want-to skills. Cross out your can-do skills, that is, any skills you can do but don't really enjoy using.

Some people ask if they have to be an expert to keep a particular skill on their list. No, if you like using a skill and have a moderate amount of experience with it—for instance, if this skill shows up in three of your five stories—keep it on your list. Remember, it's always possible to develop your skills more fully through education, practice, or concentration.

Now, the really fun part: finding your best skills. Go back to the Skill TIPs list. Of the skills that you checked (you may have checked some skills more than once), select ten that you most enjoy using. Write each one on a slip of paper or Post-it note. Look at each skill. Think about how much you want to use that skill. Do you want to use it often or only occasionally in your work? Place these skills in order from your most favorite to your least favorite. This can be hard, but give it a try. When you know your best transferable skills, you have an important clue for finding work you love.

Now, look at the top five: these are your best skills. They are an important part of your parachute. Write these five skills on My Parachute (p. v) in the section My Best Transferable Skills. (If you want, use colored pens or pencils to add a little color to your parachute!)

For a quick summary of these steps, see the Identify Your Best Transferable Skills sidebar.

Whew! You've done a lot of hard work in identifying your favorite interests and your best skills. We hope you had fun too. Maybe you learned something about yourself that you didn't know before—or maybe these exercises confirmed something that you sensed, but weren't certain of, about yourself. Now that you know what you love to do—your interests and the skills you love to use— let's take a look in the next chapter at what types of people you like to have around you when you do what you love to do.

IDENTIFY YOUR BEST TRANSFERABLE SKILLS

1. Review your list of skills used. Cross out skills you don't enjoy using.
2. Select ten skills you enjoy using.
3. Put the skills in order from most favorite to least favorite.
4. Look at your list of ten skills. The top five are your best transferable skills.
5. Write those skills in the My Best Transferable Skills section of My Parachute (p. v).

If You Want to Explore Further . . .

FINDING YOUR DREAM JOB

Richard N. Bolles, *What Color Is Your Parachute? 2006* (or latest edition). Ten Speed Press, 2005. Also check out the companion website:

www.JobHuntersBible.com

IDENTIFYING YOUR SKILLS AND PLANNING YOUR CAREER

This fun site (the website of European career expert Daniel Porot) will give you lots of information about identifying your skills, planning your career, and searching for jobs. If you want to go right to the skills section, click on the "Self-Assessment" tab at the bottom left on the home page.

www.careergames.com

EUREKA is a comprehensive career-planning and job-search website. Check to see if your high school career center belongs to EUREKA or if you can gain access to the website at a local DOL One Stop or state employment office. Individual student subscriptions are $30 a year. To get to the skills section of the website, click on Self-Assessment. This links you to a page that gives you a choice of several skill-assessment exercises. You can do just one, or do several and see what you learn from each one.

EUREKA.org

A free skills assessment that links with suggested occupations can be found at:

online.onetcenter.org/skills/

Chapter 2

who you love to work with

YOUR FAVORITE TYPES OF PEOPLE

Have you ever had a part-time or summer job where your work was actually pretty boring but you still liked going to work? If you've had that kind of job, we bet you liked going to work because you enjoyed the people there. Maybe you worked with friends, or perhaps you had a boss who was friendly and helped you learn new skills, or maybe you met interesting people—customers, clients, patients—every day. If you haven't had a part-time or summer job, maybe you've had some of these same experiences in a class. The class itself may have been boring, but you enjoyed going to class because your friends were there, or the teacher cared about you, or class projects took you outside the classroom, where you met interesting people.

Short of being a full-fledged hermit, every job you'll ever have will surround you with people to one degree or another. A good job can be ruined if you're surrounded by difficult people or people you simply aren't comfortable with, and an ordinary, not-so-interesting job can be fun if you work with people you enjoy.

Finding a dream job involves more than discovering what you love to do; it also means discovering what kinds of people you enjoy working with. Let's do that now by going to a "party"!

The Party

Imagine you've received an invitation to a party of people in their twenties where you don't know any of the people well or at all. ("What kind of party is that?!" you ask. Please bear with us, OK?) On the next page is an aerial view of the room where the party is taking place. For some reason, people with the same or similar interests have all gathered in different corners of the room.

Below is a brief list of the types of people at the party. The terms Realistic, Investigative, Artistic, Social, Enterprising, and Conventional refer to particular types of skills and the people who most enjoy using them. (For a very brief summary of these skill categories, see the sidebar entitled Who Likes to Do What—and How.) Each category includes a few examples of people who might be in that particular group. In the descriptions of these people, you'll probably notice how their interests and skills work together.

Realistic (R): People who like nature, athletics, or tools and machinery. Examples: Tom loves to hike in the mountains and does volunteer trail maintenance. Dee plays on the school soccer team. Paul repairs cars. Louise and Larry build furniture in their fathers' woodworking shop. Ross grows vegetables for the farmers' market, and Yvette raises dogs to be companion animals for people with disabilities.

Investigative (I): People who are very curious and like to investigate or analyze things. Examples: Jason always wants to know *why*—why a certain bird is no longer seen in his area, why the brain works the way it does, why one ball team plays better than another. Jessica investigates the best places to take a date—concerts, movies, amusement parks, hiking trails—and writes about them for her school paper. David analyzes everything—from the data in his chemistry experiments to the results of community service projects. Erin, a student council member, wants to figure out why new students have so much difficulty scheduling the classes they need.

Artistic (A): People who are very artistic, imaginative, and innovative. Examples: Gail draws cartoons. Sid, Don, and Stacy started a band and play at local dances. Darlene designs costumes and sets for school theater productions and is known for being able to create great stuff with few resources. Guy develops his own software for doing computer animation.

Social (S): People who like to help, teach, or serve people. Examples: Darcy, a senior, orients freshmen about life at high school. Steve tutors middle school students in math and English. Keri reads assigned class texts to a blind student. Darin volunteers as a trainer for the school football team, and Bob serves as a peer counselor.

Enterprising (E): People who like to start up projects or organizations, or influence or persuade people. Examples: Dana started a service project where high school students visit the elderly in a convalescent home. Rich, who's running for student body president, persuades people to vote for him. Greg works with kids who are at risk of getting involved with drugs and gangs.

Conventional (C): People who like detailed work and like to complete tasks or projects. Examples: Don, the treasurer for a service club, keeps detailed financial records of all their fund-raising activities. Kristin works part-time in an insurance office, where she's responsible for keeping all the files up-to-date. Terri oversees the preparations for the prom, making sure everything that needs to get done gets done.

> **WHO LIKES TO DO WHAT— AND HOW**
>
> Here's a quick way to remember what each category of skills means:
>
> **Realistic:** Do it!
>
> **Investigative:** Explore it!
>
> **Artistic:** Invent (or create) it!
>
> **Social:** Share it!
>
> **Enterprising:** Start (or sell) it!
>
> **Conventional:** Keep it going!

OK, now you know a little about the kinds of people who'll be at the party. You've just arrived and walk in the front door. (Don't worry about whether you're shy or if you actually have to talk to anyone. That doesn't matter at this party.) Now, we have three questions for you:

1. Which corner of the room would you go to first—that is, which group of people would you most enjoy talking to for the longest time? Write the letter for that corner in the box.

2. After fifteen minutes, everyone else in the corner you chose leaves for another party. Of the groups that still remain, which group would you be drawn to the most? Which people would you most enjoy being with for the longest time? Write the letter for that corner in the box.

3. After fifteen minutes, this group also leaves for another party. You look around and decide where to go next. Of the groups that remain, which one would you most enjoy being with for the longest time? Write the letter for that corner in the box.

The three letters you selected are called your "Holland Code." The Holland Code is named for Dr. John Holland, a psychologist who did research on "people environments," that is, the types of people we most like to be with. According to Dr. Holland, everyone has three preferred people environments from among these six—Realistic, Investigative, Artistic, Social, Enterprising, Conventional. By naming whom you'd prefer to be with at a party, you've identified your favorite people environment.

(Actually, the Party exercise only gives an approximation of your Holland Code, but it's sufficient for our purposes here. If you want to take a longer test to more accurately determine your Holland Code, see the resources section at the end of this chapter.)

Now, turn to My Parachute (p. v) and write your Holland Code in the section entitled My Favorite Types of People. You may also want to write a short sentence or two about these types of people. For example, if your Holland Code is IAS, you might write: "I will enjoy my work most if I am surrounded by people who are very curious and like to investigate or analyze things (I); who are also very innovative and creative (A); and who really want to help or serve people (S)."

Now, look over the traits described for each of the three groups of people you chose and see how much of this is also true of you. We often see ourselves best by looking at others. We call this the Mirror Theory. When we describe the people we would most like to be with, in many cases we have also described ourselves. As the old saying goes, "Birds of a feather flock together." What do you think? Do you see yourself in your favorite types of people?

Remember, a test can't tell you what job you should have, but it can provide ideas as you begin your search for your dream job. In the United States, there are currently about twenty thousand job titles. Technology and consumer demand create new jobs every year. Only a couple hundred jobs are included in the databases of career "assessments" or tests. Whenever you take one of these tests, such as the Self-Directed Search, use the jobs suggested as matching your interests as a place to begin your research.

MORE CLUES TO YOUR DREAM JOB

Your Holland Code, the three letters you chose in the Party exercise, not only tells you what type of people you enjoy being with, it also provides clues to jobs you might enjoy. For example, if your three letters are RIA (Realistic, Investigative, Artistic), you may find being a police sketch artist or occupational therapist of interest. If your letters are SEC (Social, Enterprising, Conventional), you might enjoy working as a self-employed wedding planner or an event coordinator.

You can explore job possibilities using your Holland Code at cacareerzone.org, where Holland Codes are given for numerous job descriptions. You can use your three-letter Holland Code to research job possibilities on many websites and in other job-hunting resources. The great thing about this approach is that you may discover interesting jobs you might never have thought of doing, or even jobs you never knew existed.

If You Want to Explore Further . . .

The Party exercise gives an approximation of your Holland Code. If you want to take a longer test to more accurately determine your Holland Code, you can take the Self-Directed Search (SDS), developed by Dr. Holland, at **www.self-directed-search.com.** The SDS online costs $9.95, and it will take you approximately fifteen minutes to complete. You'll get a personalized report on your computer screen (which you can print out) that lists the occupations and fields of study that most closely match your interests.

If you would like a quick, free online test (based on Dr. Holland's work) to find jobs you might be interested in, check out the Career Interests Game at:

www.career.missouri.edu/students/explore/thecareerinterestsgame.php

The EUREKA site provides a variety of job-search resources, including job possibilities for various Holland Codes. By paying a $30 fee, you gain access to all that EUREKA offers.

EUREKA.org

Chapter 3

where
you
love
to be

YOUR IDEAL WORK ENVIRONMENT

Your heart has its own geography, where it prefers to be. It may be by a mountain stream. It may be in the Alps. It may be in the hustle and bustle of the streets of London or New York. It may be on an Oregon farm. It may be a beach town. Or, it might be right where you are now—in your own hometown, in your own backyard, at your high school. Maybe what you'd really love to do is return there someday as a teacher.

Your heart knows the places that it loves. That's what we'll be exploring in this chapter because finding where you love to be is connected with doing what you love to do and who you want to do it with. It's an important part of being happy with your whole life, not just a small part of it. It's living your whole dream, not just half (or less) of it.

There are lots of ways to consider where you want to be. We'll explore two: your ideal work environment and your ideal community (which includes geographical location). We'll be asking you a lot of questions. You may have answers to some of them and not to others. Maybe you won't even have answers to most of the questions. That's OK. Answer what you can— we're certain you'll have some answers—and just keep the rest of the questions in the back of your mind. Questions, even when you don't know the answer, can help you notice new things or think about things in a way you hadn't thought about them before. For example, if we ask, "Would you rather work outside or indoors?" and you aren't sure, you may start to notice what types of jobs are done indoors or outdoors, or jobs that combine both indoor and outdoor work. Maybe you'd be fine working indoors all the time, but you'd want to live in an area where you could go skiing or surfing on the weekend.

Use the answers you do have as a foundation for further exploration of where you'd love to be—to live, to work, to play. Your answers will grow as you grow, as you visit places you've never been before, as you go to trade school or college, or as you experience your first job. All of these experiences will help you learn *what*, *who*, and *where* is most important in your life.

Each person's ideal working conditions are different. Let's start by exploring something you may never have thought about before: your ideal work environment and what makes it just right for you.

Your Work Environment

When you begin working, roughly one-quarter of your time each week (assuming a standard forty-four workweek) will be at your job. Your work environment needs to be one in which you not only feel comfortable but in which you can thrive. We use the term "environment" here because your ideal *where* includes more than just the location (office, laboratory, farm) where you do your work. The environment also includes, among many other things, your work space (desk, cubicle, lab space, five-hundred-acre ranch, machine shop), physical conditions (windows or no windows, natural or fluorescent lighting, noisy or quiet), atmosphere (formal, casual, amount of contact with people, working style), company size (small, large, local, national, international), and clothing (uniform, suit, jeans).

If you've already had some work experience or if you've visited various workplaces (for example, where your parents work, your doctor's office, your school), think about what you liked or didn't like. Another way to approach this is to think about where you like to study—in a quiet library or in your bedroom with the CD player on, alone or with a group, and so on. Where do you feel comfortable or uncomfortable? Where would you like to spend more time? Because the same job (or very similar jobs) can happen in many different environments—some you would love; some you would hate!—let's start exploring what's just right for you.

DISCOVERY EXERCISE

My Ideal Work Environment

Answer the questions below as best you can. Because there are a lot of questions, don't try to answer them all at once. Set a timer for ten to fifteen minutes. Answer as many questions as you can during that time. If you're enjoying the exercise when the timer goes off, set it for another ten to fifteen minutes. Another option is to answer some of the questions now, and then come back again in a week or two and answer some more. By then, you may have noticed things that you aren't aware of right now. Also, if you think of something not included here, be sure to put that on your list too.

(continued)

(continued from page 31)

LOCATION

Where would you most like to work . . .

- Indoors or outdoors?
- In an office building? a machine shop? on a ranch? at your home? somewhere else?
- In an urban, suburban, or rural area?
- In many locations or one spot (travel or no travel)?

WORK SPACE

What kind of space would you most enjoy . . .

- A cubicle in a large room with lots of other people in their own cubicles?
- Your own desk in a private office?
- Lots of variety—at a desk, in your car, at clients' locations, on airplanes, in hotels?
- A classroom, laboratory, hospital?
- Garage or workshop?
- Outdoors—golf course? ranch? barn?
- A place with everything you need—all the latest tools or technology and necessary supplies—or a place where you need to be creative with limited resources, supplies, and equipment?

PHYSICAL CONDITIONS

Do you prefer . . .

- Fancy and upscale, moderately nice, or doesn't it matter?
- Windows that open and close or a climate-controlled building?
- Natural or artificial light?
- A light or dark environment?
- Comfortable temperature or varied temperatures?
- Safe or risky?

ATMOSPHERE

Do you prefer . . .

- Noisy or quiet?
- Calm or bustling?
- Formal or casual—for example, do you want to call your coworkers "Ms. Smith" and "Mr. Jones," or do you prefer that everyone goes by his or her first name?

- Lots of contact with coworkers or very little?
- Lots of contact with the public (clients, patients, customers) or very little?
- Would you rather work by yourself with minimal contact with others or work frequently or constantly with others?
- A hierarchical setting (where the boss tells everyone what to do) or a collaborative setting (where the staff works together to determine goals, priorities, and workload)?

SIZE/TYPE OF BUSINESS

Do you prefer . . .

- Large or small? (Think about what "large" and "small" mean to you.)
- Locally owned, national chain, or multinational?
- Do you want to know all your colleagues and customers, or would you rather always have a chance to meet someone new?
- For-profit or nonprofit organization?
- Would you like to own your own business?

CLOTHING

What would you like to wear at work . . .
- A suit?
- Trendy clothes?
- Casual, comfortable clothes?
- Jeans and a casual shirt?
- A uniform (for example, military, firefighter, police officer, waiter/waitress)?
- A lab coat?
- Different clothes for different aspects of your job (for example, a suit when meeting an important client and casual clothes for regular days in the office)?
- Whatever you want to wear?
- Something else?

Write each of your answers on a small slip of paper or Post-it note, then put them in order of what is most important to you. (You may want to include one or two items from each category above—Location, Work Space, and so on.) Select the five factors that are most important to you. Write these in the My Ideal Work Environment section of My Parachute (p. v).

Your Ideal Community

Everyone has different ideas of what makes a great place to live. If you love to ski, you'll want to be within reasonable distance of the mountains. If you love to surf, you'll want to live near the coast. Another person may want to live near a lake or river, or in the desert. You may want to live near good friends or family. Or, if you have excellent foreign language skills (or because you don't have those skills and want to develop them), you may want to live in a foreign country.

And, more directly related to their jobs, some people want to work within a few blocks of a mass-transit stop. Others want to drive to work and therefore want lots of parking. Some people might want their gym or favorite coffee bar nearby, a grocery store located on the route home from work, or a park close enough for eating lunch or taking a walk. What characteristics do you want in the community where you'll live and work?

DISCOVERY EXERCISE

My Ideal Community

GEOGRAPHICAL FEATURES

Do you want to live . . .

- In or near the mountains? near the coast? in the desert? on the plains?
- In a small town (less than 5,000 people), a medium-sized city (5,000–20,000), a large city (20,000–500,000, a major metropolitan area (500,000 or larger)?
- In a rural area with a town or city within a reasonable distance or in an isolated area, far from "civilization"?

PEOPLE

What do you prefer . . .

- A good mix of age, ethnic, economic, and religious groups?
- Mostly people your own age or in your own ethnic, economic, or religious group?
- Living where you already have friends or family or in a place where everyone is new?

NEIGHBORHOOD/HOUSING

Do you prefer living . . .

- In a subdivision?
- In an apartment or condominium?
- In a single-family home that doesn't look like everyone else's?

CULTURE

What is important to you . . .

- Good bookstores, art galleries, libraries, and museums?
- Movie theaters
- Music, dance, and theater
- A local semipro or pro sports team?

EDUCATIONAL OPPORTUNITIES

What is important to you . . .

- Personal enrichment classes?
- Professional development classes?
- A college or university?

RECREATION

What would you like your community to have . . .

- Good parks?
- Bike paths, walking/hiking trails?
- Community sports leagues and facilities?

COMMUTING

What is important to you . . .

- Commute by car?
- Ability to take mass transit to work?
- Being able to walk or bike to work?

Write the answers to these questions about Your Ideal Community on small slips of paper or Post-it notes and put them in order of which is most important to you. Then select the top five characteristics and write them in the My Ideal Community section of My Parachute (p. v).

If You Want to Explore Further . . .

WORK ENVIRONMENT

If you're interested in learning more about the working conditions or environment for particular jobs, check out the *Occupational Outlook Handbook*, which can be found at this website:

www.bls.gov/oco/home.htm

GEOGRAPHICAL LOCATION OR COMMUNITY

Want to investigate places that you'd like to live? Visit this website:

www.bestplaces.net

For job listings from locations around the world, check out this website:

www.craigslist.org

If you'd like to live abroad, see Elizabeth Kruempelmann's *The Global Citizen: A Guide to Creating an International Life and Career* (Ten Speed Press, 2002). In some fields, international experience may qualify you for a higher starting salary.

Interested in checking out various geographical locations with short-term jobs? See Michael Landes's *The Back Door Guide to Short-Term Job Adventures,* 4th ed. (Ten Speed Press, 2005).

putting the pieces together

IDENTIFYING YOUR POTENTIAL DREAM JOBS

Are you ready for the next step? In this chapter, you'll begin to identify your potential dream jobs, drawing on all the hard work you did in the previous three chapters and putting all those pieces together. As you begin to identify potential dream jobs (or fields in which you are likely to find your dream job), you'll begin to see new possibilities and directions for further exploration.

Though it can be tempting, we encourage you not to narrow your options for your dream job too quickly—that is, don't lock yourself into a particular job title without looking at all the possibilities. In general, we humans are more comfortable with labels than lists. It's certainly easier to talk about job titles than to give someone a list of skills that you like and want to use. But if you focus on a job title too soon, before investigating several jobs that might use similar skills, you may not learn about work that could be a better match for your best skills and favorite interests—in other words, you just might pass your dream job by.

> I wish I would have known that there were opportunities to earn a comfortable living much closer to the types of dreams and interests that I had in high school. I was an avid lover of maps back then. Had I known that being a cartographer was an available career, I would have fervently pursued it.
>
> —Adam Hoverman, D.O., family practice physician, age 30

If you didn't have your parachute, the process of finding your dream job would be much harder. As you know, it's very hard to find something when you don't know what you're looking for! That's why your parachute is so important. The information that you've gathered on page v will help you recognize your dream job when you come across it.

Finding Your Field of Interest

At its best, a job uses both your interests and your skills. Turn to My Parachute (p. v) and take a look at My Favorite Interests. What did you write there? Sometimes the process of finding your dream job, or potential dream job, involves a little "translation," by which we mean taking your favorite interests and determining the occupational field in which they fit.

Sometimes the fields are much broader or much more numerous than you realize at first.

If one of your interests is skateboarding, your fields might be athletics, recreation, or kinesiology (the study of the principles of mechanics and anatomy in relation to human movement). If you choose the field of athletics, you might become a skateboard coach; if recreation, you might become involved with designing a skateboard park or program for skateboarders; if kinesiology, you might design skateboards that are easier and safer to use, and also more flexible for doing various maneuvers. In each case, your training and education (for example, choice of college majors, if you go to college) would vary.

Here's another example: One of Diane's interests is medicine. Because her best skills involve taking care of sick or injured people, she wants to be a nurse. But there are many types of nurses and many places in which Diane can use her nursing skills. What kind of nurse she becomes will depend on what type of training she completes, what major she chooses, and also what her other interests are. The field of medicine is quite broad. Here are some things Diane could do:

- If she wants to work with children, she could be a pediatric nurse. Pediatrics is the *field* in which she'd use her nursing skills.

- If cancer care is a strong interest, she could be an oncology nurse. (Field = oncology)

CAREER OR JOB?

In this book, we use the words "career" and "job" interchangeably. You'll find, however, that many people make a distinction between what a career is and what a job is.

For some, a "career" means work that requires more training or education, involves more responsibility (and possibly longer hours), and pays more money. Often a career follows you home, with work to do at night or on weekends.

In contrast, many people consider a "job" to be work that requires less training or education, may involve less responsibility (and possibly shorter hours), and frequently pays less money. Generally speaking, a job is over at the end of the day.

Which word—"career" or "job"—describes what you want?

- If she is most interested in emergency medicine, she could be an emergency room nurse, work on a search-and-rescue team, or be part of a Life Flight medical team. (Field = emergency medicine)

- If Diane is also very interested in recreation, she could be a nurse on a cruise ship or at a large resort. (Field = recreation)

As you can see in Diane's case, and in the case of the person whose interest is skateboarding, the same job can happen in many different environments, some of which you'd like, and some you'd hate!

Finding Your Fields of Interest

1. Turn to My Parachute (p. v) and look at the section entitled My Favorite Interests.
2. Consider each of one your interests. What are the different occupational fields where could you use your interests? Try to name at least two or three for each interest.
3. List these jobs on a separate piece of paper or in your journal. This list isn't set in stone; as you learn more about different jobs you may want to cross out some items or add new ones.

(If you need some help translating your favorite interests into particular jobs or careers, talk with your parents, school counselor, or the staff person at a career center.)

Exploring Potential Dream Jobs

Now that you've identified your fields of interest, it's time to explore some potential dream jobs. Perhaps you have a clear idea of what those jobs may be. If so, that's great. But if you don't, don't despair. Here are some steps you can take to help you discover potential dream jobs to explore:

- Show your parachute to people whose opinions and suggestions you trust. Ask them for ideas about jobs that might match your fields of interest and your skills.

- Read tons of information about different occupations. Libraries and career centers have materials about many kinds of work. Start by finding and reading this general information. Ask the librarian or career center staff to direct you to resources that will help you find jobs that fit your fields of interest and skills.

- Use Google, Metacrawler, or other search engines to find information about different jobs or careers on the Internet.

- Read magazines and newspapers and watch TV. When jobs are mentioned, which jobs interest you? Keep a list of those jobs or cut out articles on them.

- One of the best ways to figure out if a line of work is a good match for you is to talk to people who have worked in that field for a while. If you want to continue living in the same region where you currently live, there are two things you can do to find local people doing work that interests you:

> **REALITY CHECK**
>
> Among high school graduates we surveyed, 38 percent of the high school graduates we surveyed said that their knowledge of the work world was extremely limited when they graduated. They felt they would have made different career choices if they had known about a greater variety of jobs.

1. Check out the Yellow Pages of your local phone book. Start with Z and read backwards. The Yellow Pages list many of the jobs that exist where you live. Make a list of categories that have jobs you are curious about. Call the businesses listed in these categories to find someone to talk with about the jobs that interest you most. (City, county, state, and federal government agencies have jobs too. These agencies are generally listed in the front of phone books.)

2. Find the labor force projections for the county in which you live. Contact your local state employment office (every county has at least one location). These projections let you see which occupations are in greatest demand where you live (or want to live). If there are in-demand occupations that interest you, find people doing those jobs so you can get more firsthand information.

After you've gone through these steps, you should have at least two or three job possibilities to explore.

Talking to People about Their Work: Information Interviewing

Once you've gathered and read a lot of written information about potential dream jobs, your next step is to explore these jobs further by talking with people in these lines of work. By talking with them, you will learn if these jobs really interest you or not.

This informal research is called "information interviewing." (For more details on information interviewing, see chapter 8.) In the realm of jobs, we usually think of interviewing as being questioned by a potential employer to determine our suitability for a particular job. But in information interviewing, you simply ask people for information on what their jobs are really like.

Talk with the youngest people you can find who are doing the jobs that interest you the most. Often, the people you will first be referred to are those considered successful in their field. They may be fifteen to twenty years older than you. They'll have a lot of good information for you about their work, but you also need to find out how younger workers view this kind of job.

In the last several years, there have been major changes in many industries and fields. Mid- and long-term workers in those fields may have had very different experiences than those newly hired. You need to know both perspectives in order to make a good decision about a possible career.

Your parents, relatives, parents of your friends, teachers, or other adults can help you find people who have jobs you're interested in. Talk to at least three people with a particular job or career before you decide to toss it out or pursue it as a goal. Each person's experience with and feelings about the job will vary. You want to gather the most accurate information about the job that you can. By talking with more than one person, you're likely to get a more balanced view of the job that interests you.

You can do some of these interviews over the phone. It's even better, though, to interview them at their work site so you can see the work environment. (How does it compare to your ideal work environment, which you listed on your parachute?) Until you see the actual work setting for particular jobs, you won't have a complete picture of what doing each job will really be like.

Who do I talk to?

Speak with a worker actually doing the job that interests you. This person's boss may be easier to find, and you may need to talk with the boss to get connected with someone who does the job you want information about. But don't stop with the person in charge. You need to know what it's like to do the job from an employee prospective.

Will I need an appointment?

Often you will. If the jobs that interest you are in retail stores or fairly public businesses or places, you may be able to walk in at a slow time and find someone who will talk with you. "What's it like to work here?" is an easy way to get someone talking.

But if the job or organization you want to learn more about is far away or limits public access, or if the person doing the work is very busy, you'll need to make an appointment for a fifteen-minute conversation. You can make the appointment by phone.

What do I say to make an appointment?

Develop a "pitch." Write a short script to introduce yourself to the person you'd like to interview. Here's a sample:

Hi, my name is Megan. My father gave me your name because you own a mobile pet-care business. I like animals very much, and I'd like to learn more about businesses that involve pets. Could I make an appointment to talk with you about your work? I wouldn't need more than fifteen minutes of your time.

People may want to know more about you, so be ready to add information about who you are and why you want to talk with them.

What if I freeze on the phone while making an appointment?

Have your script written out and in front of you when you call. If you experience a brain freeze, quickly refer to your script.

Will someone actually see me?

Yes. Not everyone, of course, but if you speak courteously when trying to make an appointment, communicate clearly what you want from them, and show gratitude for their time, about eight out of ten people will talk to you.

In general, people love to talk about themselves. Also, most of them remember being in high school and not having a clue about how to get a job. Many of those who do talk with you will be very impressed that you're doing research to learn about jobs that will be a good fit for you. Those who are impressed will be very helpful.

And, if they like what they do, you'll probably have to work hard to keep the conversation on track so you can ask all your questions in just fifteen minutes!

When you go for the interview, be sure to show up on time and be organized. Have your questions ready, and come prepared to take notes about their answers.

Do I have to go alone?

No. You can have one of your parents, grandparents, or another adult go with you until you feel comfortable on your own. Or you could take a friend with you. (Be sure to choose one who knows how to behave in business situations and won't embarrass you.) If you want someone to go with you, though, it's courteous to ask the person you're interviewing whether it's OK for you to bring someone with you. Don't just show up with another person.

What should I ask?

You may have specific questions you want to ask, or questions may arise during the interview. That's great, but be sure you ask the following five questions, which will give you a good sense of what the job is really like and how you can get a job like this:

1. How did you get into your job? What kind of training or education did you have?

2. What three to five tasks do you do daily?

3. What do you like about your job? What don't you like about your job?

4. What do you see happening in your field of work in the next five to ten years?

5. Do you know someone else doing this (or similar) work with whom I could talk?

As you listen to the person's answers, take notes. (You can do this when you read about jobs too.) Divide the information into the same categories as those on My Parachute (p. v). For example, if you're interviewing Dr. Kelly, a veterinarian, you may start by asking her, "How did you get into your job?" She may answer, "Well, I've loved animals since I was a little kid. I always had cats, dogs, birds, horses, and all kinds of other pets. Whenever one of them got hurt, I'd calm them down, clean out the wound— if it wasn't too serious—and help them heal. I always thought it would be great to be able to help animals all the time when I grew up, so I became a veterinarian."

In her answer, Dr. Kelly told you about her interest in animals and the skills she had working with them. So in Dr. Kelly's parachute, under My Favorite Interests, you would write "animals" and under My Best Transferable Skills, you'd write "calming animals and cleaning their wounds."

Later in your interview, Dr. Kelly may mention that it's important for her to work with people who are compassionate and who love animals (My Favorite Types of People). She may also say that she chose to become a large-animal veterinarian, working mainly with horses, cattle, and sheep, because she loves to work outside (My Ideal Work Environment) and live in a rural area where people—ranchers, cowhands, farmers—work with animals for a living (My Ideal Community).

Putting the information from all your interviews in the same categories will help you compare information. Having the information in the same categories as your own parachute will make it easier for you to compare the interviewee's parachute with yours. That will allow you to see where your parachute and theirs are the same and where they're different.

One of the most important questions you can ask the people you interview is the last one: "Do you know someone else doing this (or similar) work with whom I could talk?" Dr. Kelly, for instance, might give you the name of a small-animal veterinarian, a zoo veterinarian, and a veterinary technician. By asking for names of other people to talk with, you create additional contacts. If you get two or three names from each person you talk to you'll soon have a huge resource for learning about jobs you might like. You'll also be making contacts that may be useful later on, in your job search.

Of course, it makes no sense to follow up and interview additional people when it's clear that you really aren't interested in what they do. You might decide, after interviewing Dr. Kelly and another veterinarian, that you really don't want to have to go through all the years of school and all those science classes to work with animals. But the idea of being a veterinary technician is very appealing, so you could then interview two or three more vet techs.

Once you know that a particular career or type of work doesn't match your parachute, or overlaps only a little bit, how do you find people whose work may suit you better? The Job Meter can help you ask better questions that will help you get the information you want and need.

USING THE JOB METER

The Job Meter, which is the creation of Marty Nemko, Ph.D., helps you find people whose work is closer to what you want to do. Here's how to use the Job Meter:

1. As you think about a job or listen to someone describe theirs, give the job a rating on a scale of 1 to 10 (1 = awful; 10 = perfect).

2. If you rate the job less than 9, ask yourself, "What would have to be different about this job in order for it to be a 10?"

3. If you're in an informational interview, describe how the job of your dreams differs from the job of the person you're talking with. Try to do so without sounding rude; for example, don't say, "Your job sounds really awful!" Ask if the interviewee knows someone whose job is more like what you're looking for.

A SAMPLE JOB METER

Eric is seventeen. Last week he did an information interview with Steve, a stockbroker. Eric gave that job a rank of 3 on his Job Meter. It did involve math, analysis of information, and using numbers as a reasoning tool—some of Eric's best skills. But Steve worked in a high-rise building downtown, the work environment was very formal, and his colleagues—who looked stressed-out—worked in little offices. None of this appealed to Eric.

Today Eric is meeting with his mom's cousin Leah. She's barely thirty and has her own small business as a certified public accountant (CPA). She works in an old house that's been converted into office suites. The surrounding neighborhood has big, leafy trees and a couple of outdoor cafés. Leah's workplace feels much more comfortable to Eric than the stockbroker's office. After listening to Leah describe what she does, Eric decides to tell her about the Job Meter, an idea a teacher had explained in a career-planning class. He asks Leah what rating she'd give her job.

"A 9.5," she flashed back at him. "What do you think of it?"

Eric hesitated, then answered, "Maybe a 5 or 6. My teacher said that a job needs to be at least an 8 to be a good career target."

Luckily Leah wasn't insulted. She smiled and asked, "What would have to be different about the job for it to be a 9 or 10 for you?"

"I'm not sure I want to have my own business or lots of people as clients. I think I'd like to use my math to gather information and write reports that would go to a boss or one client. And both you and Steve, the stockbroker I interviewed last week, spend a lot of time meeting new people. I guess that's to expand your business?"

"Yes. I belong to a service club, a community business group, and a women's professional organization. I review the annual taxes for the preschool my son goes to, and I've volunteered to be the treasurer for the co-op kindergarten he'll attend next year. I'd like to think I'm more subtle than wearing a button that says, 'I'm a CPA and I need your business,' but I'm constantly looking for ways to meet people who may need my services."

"I don't think I'd like that part, constantly meeting new people. I'd also like my day to be split between working inside and outdoors."

Leah thought for a while, then she said, "I've got clients who do all kinds of different jobs. Give me a week to go through my files. I also need to check with them to ask if I can give you their names. I'll find some more people for you to talk with about careers that use math."

"Thanks, Leah. I appreciate your help," Eric responded. "The more people I talk with, the more likely it is that I'll find a job that's a good fit for me."

Some people can rate a job, evaluate it, and describe how their dream job differs as they interview someone. Others need time to think over what they've heard. If you're the second type, you can call people back. Give them a description of the skills, activities, fields of interest, or working conditions that would make a job a 10 for you. To give the person you interviewed time to think of some good people for you to talk to, you could also include this information in your thank-you note (see below) and tell them you'll call to ask for their suggestions.

WRITING A THANK-YOU NOTE

After your information interview, always send a thank-you note. Why? Whenever you meet with people or interview them on the phone or by email, they give you something very valuable—their time, experience, and wisdom. Any gift of value deserves to be acknowledged. The people you interview will appreciate that you recognize the value of their time and life experience. They'll be impressed too, and most likely will be more inclined to help you again if you should need additional information in the future.

During an interview, be sure to get a business card. For interviewees who don't have one, ask for their job title, the correct spelling of their name, and the name of the company they work for. Getting this information correct shows that you've taken the interview seriously and appreciate the help the person has given you.

Here are some tips on how to write a thank-you note:

- Buy some plain thank-you notes (drugstores and stationery stores carry them) and some stamps.
- Unless your handwriting is very good, type your thank-you note and print it out.
- Keep it simple. A thank-you note can be just two or three sentences.
- Write and send your note within twenty-four hours after your appointment. A thank-you note that arrives a week later seems like an afterthought, not gratitude.

Here's an example:

> *Dear Mr./Ms./Dr. _____ :*
>
> *Thank you for talking with me yesterday about your work. The information you gave me was quite helpful. I very much appreciate that you were willing to take the time to meet with me.*
> *If I decide to become a_____ , I will probably have more questions for you.*
>
> *Sincerely,*
> *Your Name*

If the person you met with said something particularly helpful, gave you a good suggestion, or recommended another contact who's already agreed to meet with you, you may want to mention those things in your note. You can email a thank-you note too. Email is immediate and easy to read. Be sure to use your computer's spellcheck tool.

After Your Information Interviews

When you've completed your information interviews, you should have a much clearer idea of your potential dream jobs. Write the three that seem most appealing in the My Ideas for Dream Jobs section of My Parachute (p. v).

All of your hard work will not only help you find your dream job, it may also help you in more immediate ways. You can use everything you've written on your parachute– what you've learned about yourself and what you've learned from information interviews—to approach a lot of things with a new sense of focus and direction. Starting to learn what your dream job is will help you find more satisfying summer jobs, internships, or part-time work, and it may just help you choose a college major.

•   •   •   •   •

Wow! You've done a lot of good work discovering what you love to do, who your favorite types of people are, and where you'd like to work and live.

Maybe some questions still need answering, but that's fine. Those answers will come with time. We hope you've discovered some things about yourself that you didn't even know and confirmed some things you did know.

The discoveries you've made about yourself in part 1 lay the foundation for the practical steps you can take to land your dream job presented in part 3. But first, in part 2 we want to take a look at getting the most out of high school and college (if you go to college) as well as learning to set goals—all of which can be important steps on the road to finding your dream job.

If You Want to Explore Further . . .

FINDING POTENTIAL DREAM JOBS

The Occupational Information Network (O*Net Online) has full descriptions of hundreds of occupations:

online.onetcenter.org/

For an alphabetical list of jobs with comprehensive information, including salary and training requirements, check out this website:

stats.bls.gov/oco/

APPRENTICESHIPS, INTERNSHIPS, STUDY ABROAD, AND OTHER OPPORTUNITIES

The U.S. Department of Labor can provide information on different kinds of work and apprenticeships. There are over twenty-nine thousand different apprenticeship programs offered by the Department of Labor. Formal apprenticeships are unique in that you're paid to work while you learn. You must attend training classes as well. Check out this website:

careervoyages.gov

For listings of internships, apprenticeships, volunteer, and study abroad opportunities, check out this website:

rileyguide.com/intern.html

GENERAL JOB-HUNTING AND CAREER INFORMATION

This informative Canadian site has great general information about jobs and career planning:

nextsteps.org

College students have interviewed people about their jobs and how they have or haven't used their college majors. To learn what they found out, visit this site:

www.roadtripnation.com

For creative ideas to help you with your job search, see the website of Marty Nemko, Ph.D. (creator of the Job Meter):

www.martynemko.com

Click on "Columns & Articles" (upper left). Type "job search" or "job hunt" in the search box.

on the way to your future

High school students need encouragement to seek out careers that build on what they love to do already. So often salary, prestige, or ambition gets in the way of chasing after the golden key to what already motivates and inspires. Feel the freedom to go in the dIrection that your dreams move, however and wherever that freedom is found.

—ADAM HOVERMAN, D.O.,
FAMILY PRACTICE PHYSICIAN, 30

DOES it sometimes seem that the future is very far away? Does it seem that doing what you love to do is just a fantasy? Well, there *are* steps you can take to help that fantasy become reality because right now, at this very moment, you are on the way to your future. We'll look at some of the steps you can take to your future in chapters 5, 6, and 7.

In chapter 5, you'll discover ways to make the most of your high school years and use them to move you closer to finding, and enjoying, your dream job. For those of you who plan to go to college, chapter 6 will tell you how you can use those college years most productively to prepare yourself for work you'll love. Chapter 6 actually includes a lot of great information and advice for everyone, not just those headed to college. Finally, in chapter 7 you'll learn to set goals—a tool that will not only help you shape your future, but also help you through this school year too! This exploration of making the most of high school and college and learning to set and achieve goals will give you the freedom to follow your dreams and move confidently into the future and toward finding work that you'll love.

what do I do now?

Does getting a job or starting a career seem light-years away? For some of you, that almost may be true. (We say "almost" because the future always seems to come more quickly than we expect!) So, what can you do now to help you find your dream job down the road?

Just like a savvy politician, you can use your time in high school to set up a "campaign" that will help you achieve your future career goals. This campaign includes increasing your awareness of the work world, developing job-search skills, creating a career portfolio, and considering whether you want or need to go to college. We'll explore all of those things in this chapter. And, since it's good to think about what lies ahead, we'll also take a brief look at what comes after high school.

Awareness of the Work World

As you learn more about the world of work, your awareness of career possibilities and different kinds of jobs grows. All the work you've done in the preceding chapters—exploring your interests, skills, and preferences concerning work environments and people to work with, and identifying potential dream jobs—provides a solid foundation for your growing awareness.

Even without realizing it, you're probably already doing things that are helping your awareness to grow. You may, for example, be paying more attention to what people do to earn a living.

> In high school, I wish I'd known there were more options beyond doctor, lawyer, or businessperson. I also wish I'd known that you *never* have to choose what you are going to do forever. You can always change.
>
> —Alice Prager, marketing manager, 29

You may take a career interest assessment that suggests some jobs you might like but didn't know about previously. You may have older friends or siblings who have left school and started jobs that you didn't even know existed. You may notice who enjoys their work, and who doesn't.

You can also help your awareness of the work world grow by focusing some of your high school experiences—class assignments, extracurricular activities, part-time or summer work—on possibilities for your future. Let's take a brief look at some of your options.

CLASS ASSIGNMENTS

Need to do a book report? Read a book about a superstar in the industry that most interests you. Need to do a report? Pick a profession, field, or industry that interests you and do a research paper. You might, for example, research which Fortune 500 companies were started by people who didn't finish college. Need to do a presentation? Report on what you learned in preparing your parachute and conducting your information interviews. In doing a presentation like this, you not only fulfill a class requirement, you may also help your friends and classmates learn good skills for finding work they'll love.

If your school has a community service requirement for graduation, look for ways in which you can both serve your community and explore your career interests. For example, if you're interested in being a social worker, perhaps you can fulfill your requirement by volunteering at a social service agency and developing a mentor program for refugee students from different countries. Or if you're interested in politics, perhaps you could work with the Registrar of Voters and help set up a program to register students who have just reached voting age.

EXTRACURRICULAR ACTIVITIES

Besides being fun and a great way to make friends, extracurricular activities can also help you explore career possibilities and develop valuable skills. Band, choir, drama, sports, service- or interest-based clubs (for example, language, math, business, teaching), student government, and other activities can provide opportunities to test out your interests and hone your skills. For example, if you think you'd like to teach music, perhaps your band or choir director would let you rehearse a new piece of music with the freshman choir or band. Or if you'd like to be an accountant, taking on the responsibilities of treasurer for a club would allow you to track income and expenditures, create a budget, collect dues, and so on. If you're active in drama, perhaps you could write and direct a one-act play. Serving as an officer of a club, a class, or the student body will help you develop both leadership and people skills.

If you have a particularly supportive and encouraging teacher, club adviser, band or choir director, coach, or other faculty member in an extracurricular activity, talk with that person. Ask what you can do to learn more about jobs related to that activity and how you can develop skills that could be valuable in the work world.

PART-TIME OR SUMMER WORK

You may get conflicting messages about whether or not you should work while you're in high school. Some people, like economist Steve Hamilton, believe you should put all your energy into your studies and get good grades. According to Dr. Hamilton, "Students get more long-term benefit from improving their grades than they do from a job at Arby's. Employers are looking for signals that a young person is motivated and ambitious. Grades are one signal. While the money from working part-time may be tempting, as an investment in your future, using those ten to twenty hours a week to study and improve your grades will give you a greater payoff. Whether you want to go to college or straight to work after high school, improving your grades improves your career options."

Other people believe that working part-time or in the summer can help you develop important time-management and job skills as well as a sense of responsibility. In some cases, family financial circumstances may require that you need to work while in high school. If you want or need to work, use your job to develop skills that you can use elsewhere. Even better, find a job in one of the areas you're most interested in, if possible. For example, if you work in a fast-food outlet, develop valuable skills in working with the public. If you have a good supervisor, ask him or her to teach you some basic supervision skills. If you're interested in child development, look for work at a child care center. Instead of taking a part-time job just to earn money, use it to learn skills that will help you find your dream job in the years to come.

SAVVY ACADEMIC CHOICES

In high school, you have to meet certain academic requirements, but you usually have some choice as to how you fulfill those requirements—and (again, usually) you have freedom to choose your electives. Making savvy academic choices can help you keep your career options open, as well as create new ones. That can be important in helping you land your dream job. If you're certain that you'll be going to college and know what your major will be, check with your college adviser (or the college itself, if you know where you're going) to schedule the high school courses that will be most beneficial to you when you get to college. For example, taking certain AP (advanced placement) or language courses may actually fulfill college requirements and enable you to begin work on your major sooner, and maybe even finish college sooner.

But what if you're not that clear about your future? What if you don't have a definite career goal or you want as many options available for your future as possible? Here are some ideas that will help you keep your options open:

- Keep your grades up. It's wonderful if you're the kind of person who gets all As. If not, try to maintain a GPA a bit above a 3.0—that's mostly Bs, some As, and very few Cs. This GPA won't get you into an exclusive college, but it will get you admitted to many other good (and less expensive) ones. This GPA will also impress employers.

- Language skills are very valuable. In addition to English, the languages of choice in the business world are Spanish and Chinese. If you're interested in working in business, seriously consider taking Chinese if your school offers it. Spanish can be useful in many fields—teaching, social service, building and construction, and many others. If your school offers Spanish, consider taking it every year.

- If one of your goals in life is to get a really well-paying job, take math and science classes. Many of the best-paying jobs and careers rely heavily on math and science. If your school doesn't have good teachers in these areas, find a tutor or teach yourself using a self-help math book. A librarian or knowledgeable salesperson at a bookstore can give you suggestions about books that are popular and easy to use.

- Broaden your horizons by learning more about your community, your country, and the world. Through your church or a community service organization (like the Lions Club or Rotary), you may be able to find volunteer projects at home and abroad.

- Talk to adults you know and respect. Ask them how they came to do what they're doing. Find out what they like and don't like about their work. Ask if there's anything they wish they had known or done (in high school or later) that would have affected what they're doing today.

Developing Job-Search Skills and Creating a Career Portfolio

By doing the exercises in this book, you've already started developing your job-search skills, a process that will continue throughout your years of work. Particular job-search skills—resume writing, skills for information and job interviews, writing cover letters and thank-you notes—build on the groundwork you laid in the Discovery Exercises in part 1. These concrete skills will help you pursue your career goals and find your dream job. (They may even help you land a good part-time or summer job while you're in high school.) Good job-search skills make the job search easier and more efficient as well as more effective.

If your high school or public library has a career center, check it out. Career centers are good places to build your job-search skills. Find out what resources the center offers. Does it have classes on resume writing, preparing for job interviews, or writing cover letters and thank-you notes? If so, take advantage of them. Talk with the career center staff about your interests and goals. They know a lot about careers and jobs and can point you to helpful resources and opportunities. If you don't have access to a career center, use the Internet and the relevant resources and websites listed in this book.

Here are a few other things you can do to develop your job-search skills and increase your awareness of the world of work:

- Listen to guest speakers and ask them how they got into the work they're doing.

- Attend career days.

- Continue exploring job possibilities: visit friends or relatives in job settings, develop new contacts and conduct information interviews, or do volunteer work in an area that interests you.

- Attend open houses at community colleges or local universities. Tell college representatives about your interests and ask about possible majors—and prerequisites for those majors—or training programs.

JOB SHADOWING

You can learn more about jobs that fit your interests and skills by job shadowing, where you follow a person doing a particular job for a day. You might shadow a business executive, a nurse, an architect, a teacher, or an actor. You see everything they see and do: sit in on meetings, phone calls, or contacts with clients or agents; watch them work at the computer or design table; listen to how they teach math to third-graders or prepare their lines for a performance. Job shadowing gives you a real feel for what the day-to-day work is like in a particular profession or job. It also lets you experience the work environment firsthand, which helps you figure out if you'd like to work in that particular setting all the time.

Job shadowing can be either informal or formal. In the case of informal shadowing, you simply ask a parent, acquaintance, or someone you've done an information interview with if you could shadow them for a day to learn more about their work.

Formal job shadowing is usually done through a school, career center, or other organization. The National Job Shadow Coalition, for example, is a joint effort of America's Promise, Junior Achievement, the U.S. Department of Education, and the U.S. Department of Labor. Their annual shadowing day falls on Groundhog Day (February 2). Throughout the United States, students shadow workplace mentors to see what different jobs entail and how what they're learning in school relates to the workplace. Past workplace mentors include former president George H. W. Bush, former secretary of state Colin Powell, Monster CEO Jeff Taylor, and *Today Show* anchors Katie Couric and Matt Lauer. (For more information on Groundhog Job Shadow Day and job shadowing in general, see the resources section at the end of this chapter.)

Job shadowing is an excellent way to check out jobs that might match your parachute, particularly your potential dream jobs. You also may find someone who would be willing to be your mentor in a particular field. A mentor can help you recognize and develop the skills you have that will be most valuable in a particular field as well as give you guidance on the education or training you'll need, including an appropriate college major. A mentor may also provide valuable contacts for summer employment in the field while you're going to school or contacts for landing a full-time job when you're ready

It's impossible for you to pick a single job for the rest of your life—as much as you might want (or not want!) to do that. The world of work is changing too much for you to possibly choose a job that will last your entire life. The Department of Labor estimates that workers, in their lifetime, will change jobs an average of ten times and change fields three times. So we want you to use this book simply to learn what you want to do to earn a living when you leave school, whenever that is.

for that. A mentor may serve as a reference when you're job hunting and may continue to guide you in your early (and later) days on the job. A good mentor is invaluable and will share a wealth of experience, wisdom, insight, and practical knowledge with you—much of which you're not likely to learn in school.

INTERNSHIPS

Through internships, high school students can gain practical experience in a supervised setting. Generally, an internship is several weeks or months in duration so that the intern can learn specific skills or procedures. Internships at the high school level are usually unpaid, although there are some summer programs that do provide salaries. But internships aren't about money. They're about learning valuable skills that will make you more employable or provide you with firsthand information that will help you make sound decisions about your career goals. If you do well, your internship can also gain you business contacts and employment references.

Your high school guidance counselor or career center may know about formal internship programs you can apply to. Check with your local chamber of commerce. They may sponsor internships with local businesses, or they might help you set one up.

With the help of a parent, teacher, or school adviser, you can set up your own internship. Identify a local business or agency where you'd like to work. Meet with the owner or the manager for the department in which you'd like to work. Ask if they're willing to let you be an intern.

An internship proposal should be in writing. It needs to list the skills you hope to learn, the duration of the internship, the days and hours you need to be present, and who will supervise you during your internship. Employers think of internships as jobs, and you should too. If you're lucky enough to get one, show up on time and be willing to learn.

CREATING A CAREER PORTFOLIO

A career portfolio is a collection of information you've gathered on various jobs and careers as well as information on your interests, skills, and potential dream jobs. It's like your parachute but with more details. Your portfolio can be as simple as a large envelope or a file folder in which you store all the information you've gathered, or you can put your portfolio on your computer.

If you go to a high school that offers a career-planning class, you may create a career portfolio as a class assignment. If your high school doesn't have a career

THE IMPORTANCE OF OPTIONS

Less than half of those who start college finish their degree. Given the odds, it's good to have checked out other options for gaining the career preparation necessary for the work you hope to do.

class but does have a career center, ask if someone on the staff can help you create a career portfolio. Even if your school doesn't have a career center, you can still put together a career portfolio on your own. (Check out *Creating Your Career Portfolio*, by Dr. Anna Williams and Karen Hall, which is listed in the resources section at the end of this chapter.)

What goes into a career portfolio? Here are few specific things, but don't hesitate to add anything else you think is important:

- A copy of your filled-in parachute (see My Parachute, p. v)
- A list of activities, class assignments, or experiences that show your interest in different jobs
- Information on the education or training you'll need for jobs you're interested in (including recommended college majors)
- Notes from information interviews
- A list of contacts (for information interviews, job shadowing, and so on)
- Newspaper clippings or magazine articles on people who have jobs that you find interesting

Keep updating your portfolio throughout high school. You may find that your interests and potential dream jobs change as you do additional research. That's good—that means you're taking your research seriously. But always keep the research you've already done. You never know when a contact you've made or an interview you've conducted in the past may be important. And you may also find new avenues—potential dream jobs—for using your best skills and favorite interests.

DEVELOPING A THREE-PART PLAN

Another helpful thing you can do is to make a three-part plan based on your answers to the questions below. Using your parachute and the section entitled My Favorite Interests (p. v), determine your *favorite* field (the area in which you would most like to find work). Then do additional

- In our survey of high school and college graduates, 34 percent said that they wish they hadn't waited until they graduated to make career plans and contacts.

- One out of three graduates felt that if they had gotten entry-level jobs, internships, or volunteer experience in fields of their choice while still in school, they would have realized their career goals much faster.

research (at a career center, library, or online) to answer these questions:

- What entry-level job (a job you can get with a high school diploma) could I get in my favorite field that would help me get experience for better jobs in this field?

- What job could I get in my favorite field with two years (or less) of further training or education?

- What job could I get in my favorite field with a bachelor's degree or advanced training?

By the middle of your senior year (if not before), you want to know the answers to these questions. To get good answers, you may need to return to the people with whom you did information interviews. Remember that each of the questions may have more than one answer—more than one possible job. That's great. That means you have more options. Right now you want as many options as possible, and you want to know what those options are. Having just one option is very limiting. A one-option plan is like a one-legged stool—it won't work very well. When you have the answers to these questions, add them to your career portfolio.

Should I Go to College—or Not?

This question sounds quite simple, but given the realities of today's work world, it's more complex than it seems. It used to be that getting a college education generally meant that you would get a better, higher-paying job. That isn't necessarily the case anymore.

So, to make career plans today, it's important to understand the difference between higher education (college) and training. In general, "education" is a broader type of learning. For example, to get your high school diploma, you have to take certain classes—some interest you, and others don't. To get a college degree, you select a certain major. You take classes in the subject that most interests you. You're also required to take classes in other subjects to meet graduation requirements. You may or may not find these other classes interesting, though they may provide you with exposure to ideas, issues, and knowledge that may be beneficial personally or professionally.

On the other hand, "training" is more focused or specialized. Training classes teach specific skills, technology, or procedures for use in particular settings and with particular jobs.

The way in which you get your education or training is also rapidly changing. There are many more opportunities today to meet educational or training requirements online or with more flexible learning schedules (for example, weekend or night degree programs).

Whether you choose to prepare for a career or job by going to college, pursuing specialized training, or a combination of the two depends very much on what you want to do. This is where all the research you've been doing on jobs—including the education and training requirements for those jobs—pays off. It can help you make good decisions concerning your further education or training.

Look at your answers to the questions in the previous section, Developing a Three-Part Plan. For each job that interests you and that requires additional education or training, answer these questions:

- What kind of education or training was recommended by the people with whom you did information interviews?

- How long would these studies or training take?

- What will the training for higher-level jobs cost?

- How are you going to pay those costs?

According to the Department of Labor, 75 percent of today's jobs require some amount of education after high school. This is a big change from when your parents graduated from high school. Innovations, inventions, automation of manufacturing, the relentless drive for high productivity, and continuous changes in technology have created an economy where the best-paying jobs are knowledge based. In the four to six years that it takes to get a bachelor's degree, a particular technology may have already undergone two generations of change. For many employers, the degree process is too slow. They need workers with a technical skill base who can quickly learn more technical skills. Therefore, in some industries, one- or two-year technical degrees are more valued than bachelors' degrees.

Believe it or not, you don't have to go to college to become financially successful. The Census Bureau reports that in the United States, only 27 percent of adults over twenty-five have a college degree. Many people are financially successful without a college degree. In fact, a passionate interest may be a better indicator of financial success.

The late Srully Blotnick, Ph.D., decided to find out what happened to people who decided to "go for the money." He studied the career choices and financial success of fifteen hundred people, who were divided into two groups. group A (83 percent of the people in the study) chose a career because they believed they could earn a lot of money doing it. group B (17 percent of the study group) chose a career because of their passion and desire for that work. Who do you think made more money?

Twenty years later, 101 of the fifteen hundred had become millionaires. One hundred of them were from group B, those who made choices based upon passion. Only one millionaire was from group A, those who chose their career to make money. Dr. Blotnick concluded that the majority of people who became wealthy did so because they found work that absorbed their attention. Their "luck" happened because of their passion.

Now, of course, there's nothing that says you can't combine college and your passion. College can be a good place to find and develop your passion and then hone your skills for taking your passion out into the world. College can also be a good place to build a network of friends and acquaintances who can help you pursue your passion professionally.

"But I'm not sure what my passion is or what work I want to do," you say. "Should I go to college or not?" First of all, it's important that you know that you're not alone. Second, it's possible to go to college without being certain what you want to do when you get out. In most cases, the first two years are spent meeting general requirements, allowing you to explore many different subjects. That exploration may help you find your passion and identify work that appeals to you. You can then choose a major accordingly. If cost is a significant issue for you and your family, you may choose to meet those requirements at a community college.

You can also take your education in stages. Get a certificate that increases what you can earn. Work a while, then go to school for a while. You may have to do this cycle several times. This option for achieving educational goals has been chosen by students who are ambitious but not plump in the pocketbook for generations. But if you really want to attend a four-year institution for all four (or sometimes more) years and finances are a concern, be sure to check out scholarships and grants that may enable you to do just that.

It's also important to remember that college isn't just studying and going to classes. The social and cultural aspects—making new friends from different parts of the country and the world, attending special events, enjoying the arts—also have an impact on your whole life. Friends you make in college often remain friends—and potential job-search contacts—for life.

As you can see, there are many factors to consider when deciding whether or not to go to college. The answer isn't an easy yes or no. It's important to remember, though, that the choice you make today doesn't prevent you from making another choice later. If you choose to go to work right out of high school, you can still go to college later—though, if you have a family of your own, that may present a new set of challenges.

> Seventy percent of what we learn comes from challenges, 20 percent from watching others, and 10 percent from traditional coursework and reading. *Where* you go after high school, whether you go to college and which college you go to, is much less important than *what* you study.
>
> —Rich Feller, Ph.D.
> Author of *Career Transitions in Turbulent Times*

Your life and work experience—as well as your determination to go to college—can enhance your college experience. If you begin college and find that technical training is more appropriate for the work you want to do, you can switch to a technical program. However, if you've done information interviews, hopefully you've learned whether a college degree or training is the best career preparation as well as which particular college degree or type of training you should pursue. Information interviews can help you save lots of money.

Many people complete college degrees and then return for additional education years later—either to update their knowledge and skills in the field in which they work or to move into another line of work. Currently, occupational skills have an average lifetime of ten years. To stay highly employable, plan on refreshing or adding to your skills at least every five years. In some fields, you'll need to add to your skills and knowledge more often.

Another change in the workforce that may affect your career goals is that some technician-level jobs have salaries close to or exceeding professional-level jobs. If you don't mind a year or two of further study after high school but don't like the idea of four to six, check out technician jobs in fields or industries that interest you.

Remember that you always have options and choices. Even if you make what you later feel was a wrong decision, you always can choose another direction for your life and work.

Postscript: Life after High School

As we mentioned before, in today's work world, most well-paying jobs require some amount of additional education or training after high school. You can continue your studies soon after you graduate from high school or wait a couple of years. You may not be ready for college or advanced technical training now, but after a few years of work, you may look forward to going back to school. People who decide to return to school after they've worked for several years often become great students. They have valuable work and life experience, and they've become quite clear on what they want in life—so they go for it!

In choosing what to do after high school, you have many opportunities and possibilities. Here are a few:

- Travel—around the country or around the world.

- Get a part-time or full-time job and continue your education (go to a two-year or four-year school, take online courses, get a technical certificate or license, or learn a skill or trade).

- Get a part-time job and do volunteer work to learn more skills and to make contacts that will help you in your job search.

- Get any job you can to learn more about a particular field or industry.

- Check out a new city or state (or even country!) to live in.

- Begin a government apprenticeship.

- Get a fun job, even if it's not what you want for a career.

- Join the Peace Corps, State Conservation Corps, Job Corps, or AmeriCorps. Information about these organizations is available at www.bls.gov/opub/ooq/2000/fall/art03.pdf.

- Work or study abroad.

- Join the military.

Does reading this list give you more ideas? Add them to the list. What are your top three choices? Whatever you choose to do, do it with your whole heart and live your life to the fullest.

> **TIRED OF SCHOOL?**
>
> After twelve years of classes, no one can blame you if the thought of additional studies doesn't thrill you. But a technical certificate or license, which might take only a few months to finish, can greatly boost your earning potential.

If You Want to Explore Further . . .

CAREER PORTFOLIOS

Williams, Anna, and Karen Hall. *Creating your Career Portfolio*, 3rd ed. Prentice Hall, 2004. The book comes with a CD-ROM that has templates for creating an electronic portfolio. The book and portfolio supplies can be ordered from **www.learnovation.com.**

CAREERS

Eikleberry, Carol. *The Career Guide for Creative and Unconventional People.* Ten Speed Press, 1999.

Farr, Michael, LaVerne L. Ludden, and Laurence Shatkin. *300 Best Jobs Without a Four-Year Degree.* JIST Works, 2002.

Gray, Kenneth C. *Getting Real: Helping Teens Find Their Future.* Corwin Press, 1999.

———, and Edwin L. Herr. *Other Ways to Win: Creating Alternatives for High School Graduates.* Corwin Press, 2000.

Nemko, Ph.D., Marty. *Cool Careers For Dummies, 2nd ed.* For Dummies, 2001.

Phifer, Paul. *Quick Prep Careers: Good Jobs in 1 Year or Less.* Ferguson Publishing, 2003.

Young Person's Occupational Outlook Handbook, 4th ed. U.S. Department of Labor, JIST Works, 2003.

For information about high-earning jobs that don't require a bachelor's degree, check out this article:

stats.bls.gov/opub/ooq/1999/fall/art02.pdf

This very popular site includes information on career planning, choosing a college, and job hunting:

www.quintcareers.com/teens.html

For interviews with a handful of people who are tops in their field, see this site:

www.streamingfutures.com

College students have interviewed people about their jobs and how they have or haven't used their college majors. Find out what they learned at this site:

www.roadtripnation.com

The Internet Public Library's Teen Space offers valuable information on a variety of topics from lifestyle to money to careers:

www.ipl.org/div/teen/

For young people considering a military career, visit:

www.myfuture.com

This site gets you to the latest edition of the always useful *Occupational Outlook Handbook*. It lists descriptions of thousands of occupations from A to Z. Revised every two years, the handbook describes what workers do on the job. Included are descriptions of working conditions, the training and education needed, earnings, and expected job prospects in a wide range of occupations.

www.bls.gov/oco

COLLEGE: SELECTION AND ADMISSION

Asher, Donald. *Cool Colleges for the Hyper-Intelligent, Self-Directed, Late Blooming, and Just Plain Different.* Ten Speed Press, 2000.

Mitchell, Joyce Slayton. *Winning the Heart of the College Admissions Dean: How to Get into College.* Ten Speed Press, 2001.

This link will take you to the website of the College Board, the organization that administers the PSAT and SAT tests. It offers advice on getting ready to go to college, financing college, and choosing a college, as well as information on distance learning.

www.collegeboard.com/?student

This website provides links to American colleges and universities (organized by state and alphabetically by name):

www.utexas.edu/world/univ/state

For links to the home pages of all American colleges and universities as well as Canadian and other international institutions, explore this website:

www.clas.ufl.edu/CLAS/american-universities.html

For links to home pages of universities all over the world, visit this site:

www.braintrack.com/

If you're interested in colleges that feature distance learning and that grant degrees online, check out this site:

www.onlinedegrees.com/

GENERAL EDUCATION AND TRAINING

Teens with a strong Christian faith may want to check out: *Real Life Begins After High School: Facing Your Future Without Freaking Out*, by Bruce Bickel and Stan Jantz. (Servant Publications, 2000.)

The Atlantic (magazine). From 2003 through 2005, the October issue has contained their annual College Admissions Survey. The articles cover issues important to students considering going to college as well as their parents.

This Department of Labor website helps students identify training, educational opportunities, and financial aid. It also tracks occupational and industry trends and provides links with job-search services.

> **www.careeronestop.org/**

Dr. Marty Nemko, a brilliant career strategist and author of the *All-in-One College Guide,* offers numerous articles on education and training (including "Should You Go Straight to College?") on his website:

> **www.martynemko.com**

Explore post–high school learning opportunities and costs at this site:

> **www.usnews.com/usnews/edu/eduhome.htm**

See this site for explanation of various types of education after high school:

> **www.baycongroup.com/education/ed_voc_cert.htm**

INTERNSHIPS

These sites provide information on internships in general, as well as information on specific internship opportunities:

> **www.rit.edu/~gtfsbi/Symp/highschool.htm**
> **www.collegeboard.com/article/0,3868,2-7-0-8382,00.html**
> **www.microsoft.com/College/highschool/highschool.mspx**
> **www.myfuture.com/beyond/internships_all.html**

You can find additional sites dealing with internships by using any search engine. Type in "high school internships" and you'll get pages of options.

JOB OPPORTUNITIES AND INFORMATION FOR TEENS

Check out this website for job opportunities for teens:

> **rileyguide.com/teen.html**

Provided by the Occupational Safety and Health Administration (OSHA), this is the premier site for teen worker safety and health information. OSHA's mission is to help teen (and adult) workers stay healthy and safe while on the job.

www.osha.gov/SLTC/teenworkers/index.html

In the United States, restaurants and other eating and drinking establishments employ over 3 million people under twenty years of age. Many teens' first work experience is in the restaurant industry. This fun OSHA website helps youth working in the restaurant industry to be safe and healthy on the job:

www.osha.gov/SLTC/youth/restaurant/

JOB SHADOWING

For information on Groundhog Job Shadow Day or the National Job Shadow Coalition, check out this site:

www.jobshadow.org

This site helps students understand the value of job shadowing. It encourages students to experience job shadowing throughout the year. The site also gives tips to help students get the most out of their job-shadowing experiences.

www.unitela.com/activities/js/js.html

VirtualJobShadow.com is a career exploration tool for students and job seekers. Through the use of streaming video technology, VirtualJobShadow.com provides a behind-the-scenes look at life on the job. Each career profile is comprised of a "day in the life" video, interactive video questions and answers, and relevant text information so that people can make educated decisions about their future. The site also has a mentoring component that allows users to ask questions and seek advice directly from professionals.

www.virtualjobshadow.com/vjs.asp

National Disability Mentoring Day is usually scheduled every October. Students with disabilities have the opportunity to match with mentors to explore their career interests. To learn more about the program, visit these sites:

www.dol.gov/odep/programs/dmd.htm
www.dmd-aapd.org

LIFE PLANNING

Levine, M.D., Mel. *Ready or Not, Here Life Comes.* Simon and Schuster, 2005.

MENTORS

For a site devoted to web-based mentoring for teens, see:

netmentors.org

This site has general information about mentoring. Enter your zip code to find programs in your area:

mentoring.org

MISCELLANEOUS

Education in the United States emphasizes academic intelligence, but there are other kinds of intelligence. One is emotional intelligence—a set of acquired skills and competencies that predict positive outcomes in relationships at home, school, and work. People who possess these skills are healthier, less depressed, more productive at work, and have better relationships. This site offers a twenty-minute survey that measures your Emotional Intelligence Quotient (EIQ). It's fun, free, and may reveal strengths you never knew you had.

ei.haygroup.com/resources/default_ieitest.htm

To learn more, refer to: Goleman, Daniel. *Emotional intelligence: Why It Can Matter More than IQ.* Bantam, 1997.

what do I do next?

If you're ready to go to college, that's great! Hopefully you've arrived at this decision through explorations of yourself, your interests, and your potential dream jobs. If you've decided that college is for you or is necessary for your target field or job, this chapter will help you get the most out of the experience.

In previous generations, students often went to college to discover what they wanted to do, and they were generally awarded a job after graduation simply because they had a college degree. But you're living in a different world; today career preparation isn't a one-size-fits-all proposition, and a college degree doesn't necessarily guarantee employment. By doing the exercises in part 1, you've gained a big advantage over many students beginning college. You know what's important to you and what you need to do—not simply to find a job after graduation but, more importantly, to find work you love, which, for you, means getting a college degree.

College is an exciting and fun time. You meet new people, face academic challenges, and enjoy new social, cultural, and sports activities. Your college friends often remain friends for life. Also during your college years, if you remain serious about finding work you'll love after graduation, you build valuable skills and develop contacts that will enhance your professional career. Your college years can be very rich and rewarding in many ways, but they also require a new sense of responsibility—not only for your personal life but also for your financial life. Your college education is an investment in your future.

The Financial Realities of College

Perhaps it seems odd to bring up the topic of finances so early in this chapter, but the financial realities of college affect not only your life while you're in college but also if you borrow money for school expenses or accumulate credit card debt, your life after college. (And if your parents are paying for part or all of your education, it affects their lives—and possibly their ability to retire—as well.)

You know, of course, that it costs money to go to college, and most people assume that a college degree will mean increased earnings when they join the workforce. Although college graduates earn an average of $2.1 million dollars during their work life, compared to $1.2 million dollars for high school graduates, and someone with a professional degree (MD, JD, or MBA, for example) will make $4.4 million, it's important to remember that these are averages. Lifetime earnings for some people with college degrees will be more, and for others, less. At the time this book was printed, the starting salaries for college graduates with BA or BS degrees ranged from $27,000 to $52,000, depending on what area their degree was in. (Source: Estimated full-time, year-round work for 1997–99 according to the U.S. Census Bureau, Current Populations Surveys, March 1998, 1999, and 2000.)

> **SOME STARTING SALARIES FOR RECENT COLLEGE GRADUATES**
>
> Chemical engineering: 51,800+
> Electrical engineering: 49,900+
> Computer science: $47,400+
> Accounting: $40,500+
> Information sciences: 39,700+
> Marketing: $34,600+
> History: $32,100+
> English: $30,100+
> Psychology: $27,400+
>
> (Averages from 2003)

Why is it important that you know what the starting salaries are for jobs you hope to have when you leave school? Your starting salary determines how much you can afford to borrow in students loans and charge on credit cards to finish your degree or training.

Let's say that both you and your college roommate pay the same tuition, nearly $87,500. Completing your degrees takes you both five years at a cost of $17,500 per year. You each borrow $15,000 in student loans. Your roommate graduates with a degree in structural engineering. She accepts a job that has an annual salary of $50,745. Your degree is in exercise physiology. You're still deciding what to do with your degree and have no job prospects lined up—yet soon you'll have to begin paying off your loans. How does your financial situation compare with that of your college roommate? If your first job pays half of what your roommate's does, how much longer will it take you to pay off your student loans, and how will that affect where you live, what car you drive, and what you can afford to do in your free time?

College debt is a major issue for college students and their parents. About 33 percent of college graduates leave school not just in debt but in *serious* financial difficulty. (According to college officials, more students drop out of college due to debt than due to bad grades.) In today's economy, grads who don't take the time to make career contacts and select job targets *before* graduation are extremely vulnerable. (We'll look at some specific things you can do to make yourself more marketable later in this chapter.)

So how much debt is too much? A simple way to calculate an acceptable amount of debt is the two-thirds formula (see sidebar). In short, this means that you shouldn't accumulate more debt than two-thirds of the salary you expect to make your first year out of college. (Here's where the research you've done on your preferred career fields and dream jobs is particularly important. Although you may not know exactly what your salary will be, you'll at least have a ballpark figure.) If you reach that limit and you

> ### THE TWO-THIRDS FORMULA
>
> Don't take on too much debt. Most students would be smart to limit their total borrowing to no more than two-thirds of the annual salary they expect to make in their first year after college. If you're at or near that limit and haven't finished your schooling, consider transferring to a cheaper college or taking a year off to work and pay down your loans.
>
> —Liz Pulliam Weston, MSN Money Central

still haven't finished college, you should either transfer to a less expensive school or take some time off to get a job and pay down your loans.

So, with the current financial realities of college in mind, how can you make the most out of your college years, particularly in terms of finding work you'll love? As you did in high school, you'll continue to increase your awareness of the work world and hone your job-search skills. The difference is you'll do these things with more depth—and probably more focus too, because you'll be much closer to the day when you'll need to go out and use that work awareness and those job-search skills to land a good job. Now, instead of writing a report on a job you're interested in, you'll research an issue of concern in the field where you hope to find work. Let's say you want to be an infection control nurse. Instead of writing a report on what a nurse does, you'll research new techniques for infection control in hospitals— research that will be valuable when you apply for jobs as an infection control nurse after college. Your job-search skills may be put to concrete use as you seek a summer job or internship in infection control. When you do information interviews, the information you gather and the contacts you make may literally lead to a job after graduation.

But what else can you do to make the most of college? Let's look at your college career in terms of what employers look for in new employees. (Actually, *all* high school graduates, whether college bound or not, should learn these skills because they're highly valued by employers.)

A FINANCIAL REALITY CHECK

- By their senior year, college students have accumulated an average credit card debt of $2,864 spread over five different credit cards (Source: *The Atlantic*, November 2005). Paying off this amount at $40 a month at 12 percent interest (many companies charge much higher rates) will take more than ten years (Source: www.bankrate.com).

- In 2003–04, 63 percent of graduating seniors had student loans. The median amount (half the students had borrowed more, half had borrowed less) was $16,432 (Source: *USA Today*, September 15, 2005).

- About 60 percent of college students expect to live at home after they graduate (Source: Peg Tyre, Karen Springen, and Julie Scelfo, "Bringing Up Adultolescents," *Newsweek*, March 15, 2002). This is due to both debt and their failure to make career connections while in college.

WHAT ARE EMPLOYERS LOOKING FOR?

Surveys of employers in the United States report the most important employee skills as follows:

Extremely Important

Communication skills (verbal and written)

Honesty/integrity

Teamwork skills (works well with others)

Interpersonal skills (relates well to others)

Very Important

Strong work ethic

Motivation/initiative

Flexibility/adaptability

Analytical skills

Computer skills

Organizational skills

Detail oriented

Important

Leadership skills

Self-confidence

Friendly/outgoing personality

Well mannered/polite

Tactfulness

GPA (3.0 or better)

Creativity

Sense of humor

Entrepreneurial skills/risk taker

Cultivating Qualities, Developing Skills

As you select your classes, major, and extracurricular activities, keep in mind what employers look for in employees. The top five things employers want may surprise you. They are, in order of importance communication skills (verbal and written), honesty/integrity, teamwork skills (works well with others), interpersonal skills (relates well to others), and a strong work ethic. "What about GPA?" you may ask. Well, look at the sidebar "What Are Employers Looking For?" You'll see that GPA ranks seventeenth. Employers don't ignore your GPA, but they mostly see it as a measure of your persistence, commitment, and academic aptitude—how well you can jump through academic hoops. (If, however, you plan to go to graduate, law, or medical school, your GPA will be very important.) You should never ignore your GPA and just coast academically, but if you don't have a stellar GPA, you shouldn't worry that you can't get a good job. That simply isn't true. Do your best academically—and also work on cultivating the qualities and developing the skills that employers *do* consider to be the most important.

COMMUNICATION SKILLS

Excellent verbal and writing skills—being able to clearly and concisely express thoughts, ideas, issues, problems, and so on—make it possible for you to communicate well with colleagues, the public, or clients. Even if your job focuses primarily on numbers—perhaps you want to be an accountant— you'll need to be able to clearly report the meaning of those numbers, express the outcome of an audit clearly to your clients, and indicate what they need to do to be in compliance with specific accounting procedures.

If writing and speaking come easily to you, great. Keep using and developing those skills. If you have difficulty writing or speaking, seek out help in improving these important skills. Take a speech class (you can always give a speech on the work you want to do) or consider joining a local Toastmasters group. Take an English class that requires writing and ask student assistants to help you improve your work on assignments. If your college has a learning center that offers help with studying, writing, using a computer, and other important skills, take advantage of the resources there.

Writing well and speaking well take practice. Find ways to get the practice (and the help) you need. Don't be embarrassed to ask for help with developing these very important skills. The fact that you know you need help and seek it out reveals a great deal of maturity and a strong sense of responsibility—qualities that will stand you in good stead no matter what you do.

HONESTY AND INTEGRITY

The qualities of honesty and integrity are tightly interwoven and are critical to the development of trust. Employers want employees they can trust, just as clients, customers, or patients want to be able to trust the people to whom they give their business, their money, or themselves. Being honest means you act and speak truthfully. People of integrity are real and authentic:

basically, what you see is what you get. They don't pretend to be something or someone they're not. Integrity demands that you take responsibility for your actions (or inactions), words, and life.

We all fall short at one time or another with being honest or having integrity, and we all need to keep working toward making these qualities the foundation of our interactions with other people. If you find that you have particular difficulty being honest or acting with integrity, seek out assistance through your college counseling center, a trusted adult, or a spiritual adviser.

TEAMWORK SKILLS

Most jobs demand some level of teamwork—working cooperatively with others. If you've ever worked on a class project with a team and one person wanted to run the whole show, you know how frustrating it can be. In the workplace, lack of teamwork is not simply frustrating, it's also costly for the employer.

Seek out opportunities to work on a team. You may do this with class projects or in extracurricular activities such as athletics, drama, journalism, or student government. If you have the opportunity to take a class or workshop in conflict resolution, do it. Your ability to work well with others is a skill that will enhance any workplace (as well as any classroom, dorm room, or family situation).

INTERPERSONAL SKILLS

Because most jobs involve ongoing contact with others— colleagues, clients, customers, students, and so on—being able to relate well to people is an important skill. Sometimes interpersonal skills are simply called "people skills." These are skills like being able to make conversation with strangers, welcoming people into new settings, resolving conflicts, and listening to the concerns or problems of others.

Interpersonal skills come quite naturally to some people and are more of a challenge for others. If they're a challenge for you, watch people to whom these skills come easily. See if you can adopt some of their ways of relating to people. Check with the career center at your college to see if they—or the counseling center—have resources or resource people who can help you build stronger interpersonal skills.

Throughout your college years, take opportunities to develop these skills. Be a dorm proctor or adviser. Serve in student government, on the dorm council, or as a club officer. Give tours of the campus for prospective students. Work with children—and their parents—at the college child care center. Like many other skills, people skills take practice—and using them can be fun!

STRONG WORK ETHIC

A strong work ethic may mean different things to different people, including different things to different employers. In general, though, a strong work ethic means that you're willing to work hard; you're dependable, responsible, and punctual; and you take seriously the work you do for your employer, and you do that work as well as you possibly can.

As you do your information interviews and job shadowing in college, observe the work ethic in operation at each place of business. Be aware that what's expected at one place of employment may not be expected at another. You need to find a good fit between your own work ethic and that of your employer. (That's why, when you have a job interview, you're actually interviewing the employer as much as the employer is interviewing you. You want to see if this is a place where *you* want to work, just as the employer wants to find out if you're the person they want and need.)

Let's say you want to be a software developer. In your personal work ethic, you're committed to working hard and conscientiously, but you also want time to relax, be with your family and friends, and pursue other interests. You wouldn't fit in well at a company where you're expected to work eighty hours a week, never take a vacation, and spend any free time you might have talking with colleagues about work.

Your commitment to your college education is an indicator of your work ethic. (This is one place where your GPA may reveal qualities an employer considers valuable.) In general, if you're serious about getting as good an education as possible, you'll study hard and be dependable, responsible, and punctual (that is, you meet course requirements and don't cut classes or show up late). You'll take your academic work seriously and do your work as well as you possibly can. If you need help with study skills, see if your college has a learning resource center. Utilize department assistants or tutors if you need them. If you're having difficulty with a particular class, talk with the professor or teaching assistant to see if you can get some additional help. Your initiative in getting help indicates a good and healthy work ethic.

Ways to Gain Experience and Develop Contacts

In addition to developing the qualities and skills that employers want most, it's important to use your college years to gain work experience and develop contacts that will be useful to you when you interview for jobs. Information interviews, job shadowing, and internships (sound familiar?) are good ways to gain experience and develop contacts.

INFORMATION INTERVIEWS AND JOB SHADOWING

Continue with doing information interviews as you did in high school, but now do them in more depth. (To review information interviewing and job-shadowing techniques, see chapters 4, 5, and 8.) Ask to meet with people for thirty minutes and ask for more detail about the day-to-day realities of their jobs and the direction they see their career field going, including what opportunities or obstacles that might present for you.

Chapter 5 offered some basic information about job shadowing. You can use the same technique in college to learn more about particular jobs. With additional life, academic, and possibly work experience, you'll be better able to use the experience to assess whether a particular job is suitable for you.

Ask the staff at your college career center for help in finding people (perhaps alumni) for you to job shadow or interview. Faculty members in the area of your major, as well as your college roommates and friends (and their parents), may also provide important contacts. Contact your college's office of alumni relations. Most schools have databases about their grads that include employment information. And don't forget those people you job shadowed or did information interviews with when you were in high school. If your interests still lie in the same area, contact them again to see if they might be willing to be shadowed or interviewed again—this time in more depth.

INTERNSHIPS

Many companies and businesses offer internships to college students. Some are paid and some are not; some take place during summer, others during the school year. Internships are designed to introduce you to working in a particular field or job, and to give you practical work experience. For example, let's say you want to be a magazine staff writer. A magazine may offer a summer internship program that introduces you to the publishing world, allows you to work with a staff writer, and gives you a writing assignment to complete before the end of your internship.

Internships are a great way to check out a job or field that you're very interested in, and they look good on your resume. If your experience is a good one, you may be offered a full-time position at the business where you interned following graduation, or people you worked with may offer to write professional references for you or provide contacts with potential employers.

Check with the career center at your college for information on internships. (Also see the resources section at the end of this chapter.) If you're unable to find an internship that fits your particular needs, try contacting a company that you're interested in working for to see if you can set up an internship.

> **IMPORTANT TIP**
>
> When you finish an internship, volunteer project, or job in which you have done well, ask for a letter of recommendation before you leave. Even if your supervisor or professor likes and remembers you, he or she may have trouble remembering the details of your work after even six months. These letters can be important as recommendations for both jobs and graduate school.

Though our focus in this book is helping you find work you'll love, you undoubtedly already know that life is more than just work. The college experience, in addition to providing you with academic grounding for your life's work, also challenges you to discover what you truly value and to find a way to balance the many different aspects of your life. If taken seriously, the challenges and responsibilities that you didn't have to worry much about while you were living at home will help you grow and mature: learning to work out differences with roommates, facing new financial realities (such as using credit and student loans wisely), balancing study time with social time and perhaps work obligations, and maybe maintaining an apartment (cleaning, grocery shopping, and cooking). If you ignore them, you'll waste not only a lot of money but also your opportunity to be better prepared for finding good and satisfying work after college. The new life experiences of college can develop important skills that will help you when you join the work world.

But most of all, enjoy yourself! No time in life is quite like your college years. Have fun, learn as much as you can, and continue building a strong foundation of skills to help you find work you'll love.

If You Want to Explore Further . . .

CAREERS

Coplin, Bill. *10 Things Employers Want You to Learn in College: The Know-How You Need to Succeed.* Ten Speed Press, 2003.

Visit this fun website to find out how people have actually used their college education:

www.roadtripnation.com

This website for college students with entrepreneurial interests includes interviews with people who have started their own businesses. The site's founder also wants to encourage students struggling with career choices.

www.themomentumjourney.org/Intropage.htm

This site offers a variety of career information, including a link to a career quiz:

www.princetonreview.com/cte/

Geared to college students and alumni, this site lists both jobs and internship opportunities:

www.monstertrak.com

Visit the career centers at various universities around the world here:

www.careerresource.net/carserv/

Designed for the University of Waterloo (Canada), this site's comprehensive six-step *Career Development eManual* includes downloadable worksheets:

www.cdm.uwaterloo.ca/

For an article about the current decline in jobs for college graduates, go to:

www.bearcave.com/misl/misl_other/college_grad_unemployment.html

COLLEGE: SELECTING MAJORS OR TRANSFERRING TO ANOTHER SCHOOL

Freedman, Eric. *How to Transfer to the College of Your Choice.* Ten Speed Press, 2001.

If you enjoyed the Party exercise in chapter 2, check out this site that uses your favorite types of people—Realistic, Investigative, Artistic, Social, Enterprising, or Conventional—to help you find possible college majors:

www.self-directed-search.com

This site lists careers in thirty industries and the majors needed to pursue those careers:

www.collegeboard.com/csearch/majors_careers/profiles/index.html

COLLEGE: SURVIVING AND THRIVING

Carter, Carol. *Majoring in the Rest of Your Life: Career Secrets for College Students.* LifeBound, 2005.

Combs, Patrick. *Major in Success.* Ten Speed Press, 2003.

Tyler, Suzette. *Been There, Should Have Done That: 505 Tips for Making the Most of College.* Front Porch Press, 1997.

———. *Been There, Should Have Done That II: More Tips.* Front Porch Press, 2001.

Readers in the U.K. have access to the way-cool book *If I'd Only Known*. The book is a guide for students and parents to help them make the most of higher education. Readers from other countries may download the book at:

www.agr.org.uk/publicationlibrary/view_report_summary/id.41.html

For an article on the limits of more education, go to:

www.epinet.org/content.cfm/webfeatures_viewpoints_education_limits

FINANCIAL REALITIES

Avoiding Debt

Internet articles on avoiding debt can be reached through the links below:

To find out how much college debt is too much, check out this site:

moneycentral.msn.com/content/collegeandfamily/Cutcollegecosts/
P36836.asp

To understand why many young Americans are drowning in debt, check out this site:

moneycentral.msn.com/content/collegeandfamily/Moneyinyour20s/
P101676.asp

For information on saving money on your student loans and cutting college costs, visit this site:

moneycentral.msn.com/content/collegeandfamily/cutcollegecosts/
p36839.asp

What are the top ten shocks for college grads? Find out here:

moneycentral.msn.com/content/collegeandfamily/Moneyinyour20s/
P85589.asp

Many college graduates start out with a staggering load of student loan and credit card debt. Visit this site to learn smart strategies for tackling debt:

moneycentral.msn.com/content/collegeandfamily/Moneyinyour20s/
Moneyinyour20s.asp

For three ways to avoid the student loan trap, check out:

moneycentral.msn.com/content/Savinganddebt/Managedebt/
P107758.asp

If the links above have expired, go to MSN Money and search using the phrase "college debt" or "student loan debt."

Financial Literacy

This fun site is geared to teens:

www.ntrbonline.org/

On this website, click "Watch the trailer" for a video on financial literacy that's both humorous and informative:

www.masteringmoney.org/

INTERNSHIPS

For listings of internships, apprenticeships, volunteer, and study abroad opportunities, check out these sites:

rileyguide.com/intern.html
www.thejobresource.com/jobseekers/internships/
www.quintcareers.com/grad_internships.html
www.campusinternships.com/

For more information on internships, do an Internet search using the phrase "college internships."

a tool to shape your future

SETTING GOALS

As you've been reading through the previous chapters, completing the exercises, and answering questions, you've been gathering information on your interests, skills, and potential dream jobs. You've seen how you can use your high school and college experiences to enhance your job readiness and awareness of the work world. Now we'd like to introduce you to a simple tool that will help you shape your future: goal setting.

The *Merriam-Webster's Collegiate Dictionary* (eleventh edition) defines "goal" as "the end toward which effort is directed: AIM." More simply, a goal is something you want to achieve or accomplish: learning to drive a car, getting a high school or college diploma, or being elected student body treasurer. A goal can also be to experience something you dream of: traveling to India, going white-water rafting, or meeting an uncle you've never met. Some of your goals may be personal, such as getting to know someone better, reading a particular book, or learning to get along with your little sister better; others may be academic, like getting into a particular college or work-training program, earning a 3.0 GPA, or surviving chemistry. Still others, like finding your dream job, may be work-related. Because life is about more than just school or work, your goals also may relate to anything—relationships, learning experiences, and just simply having fun.

Goals help us in at least two ways: first, they articulate what we really want to do (that is, what we consider most important to do), and second, they help motivate us to do what we say we want to do! Just writing goals down makes them more concrete. When we say we want to do something "someday," that "something" and "someday" remain very vague, and more often than not, we never get around to doing it.

To give your goal-setting muscles a little practice, here's a quick exercise in naming your goals.

A Quick Exercise: Goal Setting

Take a sheet of paper. Turn it so that the long edge is horizontal and fold it into three equal sections. At the top of the first section, write "What I hope to do in my life." At the top of the next section, write "Things I hope to do in the next three to five years." At the top of the last section, write "Things I want or need to do in the next six months."

Set a timer for two minutes (or have a friend time you). Start with any column. Write down anything that comes into your head during those two minutes. After two minutes are up, set the timer for another two minutes and turn to one of the other columns. It makes no difference which one you do next. Complete all three sections. This whole exercise will take you just six minutes.

What do you think about the things you've written? Are there any surprises? Were any sections more difficult to complete? Just thinking about things you want to accomplish may stimulate other ideas over the next few days. Add them to your list. When your list feels complete, pick three goals that you want to accomplish in three to five years, and then choose three lifetime goals. Write these goals at the center of your parachute (see My Parachute, p. v).

Choosing Goals

Goals have different timelines. For example, you may find it helpful to set three-month or six-month goals—or goals for your academic term. You may have papers to write or projects due during this time. For any given goal, if you make a list of what you need to do month by month or week by week, you can achieve your goal without cramming in all the work at the last minute.

For longer-term goals, such as lifetime goals, you'll probably want to take more time to think about them. It's important to remember that your goals reflect your values. When you think about your goals, ask yourself these questions:

- What is important to me?

- What do I most want to do with my time on earth?

These are not always easy questions to answer, but they're important to think about. Some of your goals may change over time, while others become clearer. Whenever you accomplish a goal, find another one to take its place.

Moving toward Goals: To-Do Lists

Once you begin to articulate your goals, it's important to plan how you're going to accomplish them. A good way to do this is the simple to-do list.

Let's say that one of your goals is to attend a particular college or art school. Here's what your to-do list might look like:

1. Check out the school's website for admissions and application information.
2. Register to take the SAT (or other admissions tests).
3. Talk to a college admissions counselor about high school courses I should take.
4. Register for those courses.
5. Take the SAT.

Maybe as you're working your way through your to-do list, you learn that, because you're going to an art school, you don't have to take the SAT, but you do have to prepare a portfolio for the admissions process. In that case, you'll revise your to-do list to look something like this:

1. Find out the explicit requirements for the portfolio.
2. Talk to the admissions counselor about portfolio requirements and high school courses I should take.
3. Begin assembling my portfolio.
4. Complete my portfolio by the application deadline.

When preparing your to-do list, think of it as breaking down your goal into very manageable steps. If you make the steps too big, you may get discouraged. If the steps are just the right size, you'll keep moving toward your goal. If you find that you keep avoiding your to-do list, maybe the steps are too big. Take one step and break it down into two or three smaller steps.

Each time you complete a step, check it off. Completing a step is an accomplishment in itself—you're on your way to achieving your goal!

Reevaluating Goals

As you move toward your goal—particularly long-term goals—you'll have new experiences and gather new information, both about yourself and about your goal. New experiences and information will help you evaluate that goal. What you learn may confirm that a particular goal is the right one for you, or your experiences may lead you to revise your goal to include new ideas or new life directions. Depending on what you learn and what your experiences are, you may even want to abandon one goal and adopt another one that's more appropriate.

A Tool for Life

Goal setting isn't something you do just once. You'll continue to set goals (and develop to-do lists to accomplish those goals) all your life. Knowing how to set and achieve goals, then, is a very important life tool. By the goals you set, you shape your life.

Writer Annie Dillard once said, "How we spend our days is, of course, how we spend our lives." How do you want to spend *your* life?

If You Want to Explore Further . . .

Bachel, Beverly K. *What Do You Really Want? How to Set a Goal and Go for It! A Guide for Teens.* Free Spirit Publishing, 2001.

You'll find a number of Internet sites on goal setting if you do a search. Type "goal setting, teens" in the search box. Some links go to commercial sites that want you to buy products. Some sites have free information.

landing your dream job ...and more

I wish that someone would have told me that success comes more easily if you are doing a job that you truly enjoy and not to pursue a career that seems "safe" if it is going to make you miserable. People have said that forever. Apparently this needed to be pounded into my head.

—JULIE PORTEOUS LEACH, AUDITOR, AGE 29

ARE you ready to learn how to land your dream job . . . and more? Great! All the work you've done in the earlier chapters of this book provides a foundation for this next important step. In part 1, you became a detective in your own life, finding clues that revealed your dream job (or field) through identifying your interests, best skills, favorite types of people, and ideal work environment. In part 2, you explored ways to continue the journey toward your dream job by making the most of high school and college (if you choose to go), as well as setting short-term and long-term goals.

Now we'll dive into the depths of job hunting, where we explore concrete ways to make your job hunt more efficient, effective, and successful (chapter 8). Next, we look at the top ten mistakes job hunters make—and how *you* can avoid them (chapter 9). Finally, in closing, we'll put the search for your dream job in the larger context of your whole life. We'll invite you to consider who you want to be, what you most want to do in life, and how you can use your talents to make the world a better place to live.

Chapter 8

how to search for— and find —your dream job

Job hunting is both exciting and scary, and probably a few other things as well! But if you've carefully prepared your parachute and named your interests, skills, and preferred work environments and type of colleagues, you'll be far ahead of most people beginning the job search. Because you've started cultivating your awareness of the work world and developing job-search skills (such as information interviewing) in high school, you have a good springboard for diving into the actual job hunt—and finding your dream job.

Good Job versus Dream Job

Let's consider, just for a moment, the difference between a "good" job and a "dream" job. A good job is a job that you enjoy most days, that pays well (given your level of skill and the going rate in the marketplace), and that uses many of your best skills. A dream job, on the other hand, is one that you love. You'd do it even if they didn't pay you well. But in a dream job, the pay is good (again, considering both your skills and the marketplace). The job uses 75 percent of your best skills, incorporates your interests, and expresses your values. (The identification of these factors as vital to career satisfaction comes from longtime Parachute practitioner Deeta Lonergan.)

> **FOUR STEPS TO YOUR DREAM JOB**
>
> Step 1: Conduct information interviews.
> Step 2: Cultivate contacts and create networks.
> Step 3: Research organizations of interest.
> Step 4: Begin your campaign to get the job you want.

We are not using the term "dream job" to describe a fantasy job that you don't have the skills or temperament for; for example, you dream of being a trauma surgeon but you can't stand the sight of blood. We're also not talking about unrealistic goals where you do have some of the needed skills, but it would be nearly impossible to achieve your dream. Even if you excel in basketball, it's very unlikely that you could sign with an NBA team after the ninth grade—something no basketball player has yet achieved.

A dream job is one that you *can* get. It may take you a few years and some hard work. But by planning, getting the right education or training, and making contacts in the field, and with some luck, you can land that dream job.

Steps to Your Dream Job

Now we'll walk you through the steps, some of which will be familiar, that will help you land the job of your dreams.

STEP 1: CONDUCT INFORMATION INTERVIEWS

Assuming that you did the exercises in part 1 on the road to identifying your potential dream jobs or particular areas of interest, the first step as you look for your first full-time job is information interviewing. You learned the basics of information interviewing in chapter 4, and now you'll build on those basics. Information interviewing isn't complicated. It's just a conversation

---

WHY SHOULD I DO INFORMATION INTERVIEWS?

Information interviews help you find and then get your dream job. Here are the five top reasons for doing information interviews:

1. You confirm that a certain job is the one you want. An actual job can be quite different from a written job description.
2. Information interviews take the terror out of hiring interviews because you learn how to talk with a professional about the job you're interested in. (Counselors report that it takes teenagers approximately nine information interviews to become comfortable talking with adults about work.)
3. You learn what parts of your experience, training, and education make you a strong job candidate. Knowing that, you can talk about yourself in a hiring interview in a way that will convince your interviewer that you're the right person for the job.
4. Doing information interviews lets an employer see that you're willing to take initiative and responsibility. Both traits are highly valued by employers. (Because of your initiative—as well as your skills and interests—you may find yourself being considered for a job that wasn't even advertised.)
5. Information interviewing can provide you with knowledge that offsets your lack of work experience.

---

with another person about a shared interest or enthusiasm—in this case, a particular job or career. Let other people tell you their stories about how they came to do the work they do—work that you are also interested in doing. Once you've talked to several people, you'll know:

- If this is a good career choice for you

- More about the industry or field this job is in

- Common salaries for this work

- Employers who hire people to do this work

- Ideas for how you can train for or get such a job

Information interviews will reveal whether or not your best skills match the most common activities or tasks done in a particular job.

In this first step, find and talk to people who have jobs or careers that interest you. (These interviews are in addition to ones you may have done earlier, in high school, when you were just beginning to research jobs and careers.) If you've targeted three to five potential dream jobs, continue your research by talking with people who do the job you want to do or who work in the same field for each of your dream jobs. These conversations will help you determine how well each target matches your parachute. The job that matches best will become your #1 job target, the job that matches next best becomes your #2 job target, and so on. Try to find at least three kinds of jobs or careers that overlap with your parachute.

Let's say you're interested in the arcade and family entertainment business. You would arrange to interview someone working in that field. Tony's profile (page 104) is an example of what you might learn in your information interview. You will find additional profiles—of an actress, computer animator, medical doctor, computer network administrator, sportswear sales representative and manager, software engineer, tattoo equipment sales representative, and teacher—in the appendix. These profiles show you how much important information you can glean from an information interview. They introduce you to different jobs and different types of people. The jobs cover a range of education and training requirements, and represent a range of salaries. Some of these people feel they have a dream job. Others feel they have a good job. All those profiled enjoy their work.

When you ask the same questions in interviews with various people, you get very different information, and seeing these differences can be very helpful. (You'll probably notice that the interview questions in this chapter—while related to those in chapter 4—go into more depth and will help you get a better idea of whether or not a job is a good fit for you.) After you've done several information interviews, you'll be ready for step 2.

BASIC INFORMATION INTERVIEW QUESTIONS

1. What do you do? What are three to five of the most common tasks or activities you do each day?
2. How long have you been doing this work?
3. How did you get into this work?
4. What kind of training or education did you need for this job? How much did it cost?
5. What do you like about your job? What don't you like about your job?
6. What are the main challenges in this industry?
7. What do you see happening in this field in the next five to ten years?
8. What is your ultimate career goal?
9. What is the starting salary in this job or field? What is the salary range with three to six years experience?
10. Do you have any additional comments, suggestions, or advice?
11. Can you give me the names of two or three other people who do this same work?

ARCADE/FAMILY ENTERTAINMENT

NAME: Tony Tallarico   **AGE:** 31

JOB TITLE: Director of Fun World Operations

FIELD(S): Arcade/Family Entertainment

EMPLOYER: John's Incredible Pizza

DEGREE: Bachelor's in political science

TRAINING: Technical/industry-specific training (basic electronics and Randy Fromm Arcade School)

COST OF EDUCATION AND TRAINING: $120,000

SALARY: Entry-level technician—approximately $7–10/hour; technical/operations manager: up to $35,000; executive level: up to $60,000

WHAT DO YOU DO?

I oversee the development, installation, and operations of large arcades and game rooms. My typical activities include planning and development of new facilities from 15,000 to over 50,000 square-feet in size. Game rooms featuring video and redemption arcade games, rides, laser tag, bumper cars, and miniature golf; technical support and repair of games, rides, and attractions; equipment evaluation and rotation between locations; merchandise selection, pricing, and display; and evaluating overall facility operations.

HOW LONG HAVE YOU BEEN DOING THIS WORK?

This is my first year with John's Incredible Pizza. Prior to that, I spent five years with Jillian's Entertainment Corporation and five years with Dave & Buster's, Inc.

HOW DID YOU GET INTO THIS WORK?

My career started accidentally as a part-time job shortly after college. I began by helping set up a large facility prior to opening—unloading games off of trucks and installing equipment. Once the facility was open, I helped maintain the equipment (doing cleaning and minor repairs). I also assisted guests with the game room (game problems, prizes, game play, and so on). I continued to learn the technical side of the industry in order to repair the equipment and work on the systems related to them (such as card readers and computer networks). From a management standpoint, I continued to learn how to oversee the larger and larger staffs that were required to run several areas of amusement and entertainment venues. Of course, I had to learn the arcade gaming industry to know what machines were profitable and reliable.

WHAT KIND OF TRAINING OR EDUCATION DID YOU NEED FOR THIS?

Starting out as a technician, it's best to enroll in a technical school or community college to get some theory. However, there is no substitute for the hands-on experience that can only come from working on equipment in the field. Although today's video games are becoming more and more PC-based, unlike the earlier proprietary systems, you still need to be able to troubleshoot and perform repairs down to the component level to be truly successful. Also, there is a fair amount of mechanical expertise needed to work on some of the larger equipment (such as ride simulators, bumper cars, or bowling lanes) in a facility. You have to get your hands dirty and pay your dues before you get to fly to Las Vegas and play with the newest arcade games and rides!

WHAT DO YOU LIKE ABOUT YOUR JOB?

The ability to create an environment where people can go to forget about their daily worries and have fun!

WHAT DON'T YOU LIKE ABOUT YOUR JOB?

Retail is a very demanding field. Our busy time is when everyone else is off: nights, weekends, holidays.

WHAT DO YOU SEE HAPPENING IN THIS FIELD IN THE NEXT FIVE TO TEN YEARS?

The coin-operated arcade industry is shrinking due to the advent of powerful home systems (PlayStation and Xbox platforms). Smaller operators of arcades are being pushed out, and facilities are becoming increasingly larger in order to offer more entertainment options under one roof.

WHAT IS YOUR ULTIMATE CAREER GOAL?

To have ownership interest in a family entertainment facility.

TONY'S ADDITIONAL COMMENTS

Over the last ten years, I've been involved in the opening of over twenty-five facilities, averaging about 50,000 square feet apiece and costing $10,000,000 each. I've had the opportunity to travel to every major market in the United States, as well as some international markets.

This job is exciting because it combines hard skills, such as technical expertise, with the soft skills required to deal with employees and guests. In addition, I also keep up on merchandise, arcade, and entertainment trends in order to continue to maximize the income of our operations. I'm lucky that I work at a job that doesn't require me to sit behind a desk all day long, and one that provides entertainment for millions of guests each and every year. I know I've done a good job when it appears that I'm not needed—because the games, the facility, and the employees create an experience that lets the guests forget about their problems and keeps them coming back.

STEP 2: CULTIVATE CONTACTS AND CREATE NETWORKS

The people you meet through information interviewing become part of your career network. These people—like people you know—become contacts for the future. Together your contacts make up a network. You have a personal network—friends, family, and other people you know—and a professional or work network—people whose work is the same or similar to what you're interested in doing. Both networks can be helpful in your job search.

> **DON'T FORGET THE THANK-YOU NOTE**
>
> ---
>
> Never underestimate the value of thanking someone for taking time to meet with you. (To review the basics of writing thank-you notes, see page 48.)

Here's an example of how contacts and networks work: One of your parents' friends (personal network) suggests that you talk to a local banker—not because you want to be a banker, but because she knows a lot about businesses in your area. You have a good conversation with the banker, learn what you need to learn from her, and send her a thank-you note after the information interview. Some time later, you want to talk with someone in the construction industry because you're interested in becoming a building contractor. A natural place to start would be with this banker, who is now a contact of yours (professional network). If she doesn't personally know a building contractor with whom you can talk, she's likely to know someone who can make that connection for you.

Contacts become your extra eyes and ears. They may hear about job openings before they become public and alert you to those opportunities. They can help you with specific information you may need—for example, when you want to do an information interview and you can't find someone who does exactly the type of work you're looking for. Later, when there's a job you're particularly interested in, they may be able to help you get an appointment with the person responsible for hiring for that job. Or, if the job is at the same place where your contact works, he or she may be willing to act as a reference for you. Since employers highly regard the recommendations of their colleagues and employees as to whom they should hire, creating a network of people who do what you want to do is a valuable investment of your time and effort.

It's important to keep the contact information of people you meet—names, phone numbers, and addresses (both email and snail mail) so that you can utilize their expertise (and their contacts) in the future. Keep this information in your career portfolio (see chapter 5).

You can also get names of people to contact from:

- People with whom you've had information interviews

- Members of community service organizations (such as the Lions Club, Kiwanis, Rotary, and Soroptimists)

- Printed material: the business section of your daily paper or its archives, a company website, through Internet research, or annual reports or public relations articles compiled by companies themselves

- People you've met through temporary or volunteer work

We'll return to your contacts and networks a little bit later in this chapter when we look at how to begin your campaign to get hired for a particular job (see page 110).

BUT I DON'T HAVE ANY CONTACTS . . .

You probably have more contacts than you realize. Here are a few:

- Family—immediate and extended

- Friends and parents of friends

- Neighbors

- Coworkers and employers (past and present)

- Teachers or professors

- School guidance counselors or club sponsors

- Your pastor, rabbi, mullah, youth group leader, or other members of your spiritual community

- People you meet in line at the movies, grocery store, or on vacation

- Mentors or people you've job shadowed

STEP 3: RESEARCH ORGANIZATIONS OF INTEREST

Now that you've done your information interviews and prioritized your job targets (step 1), and started cultivating contacts and creating networks (step 2), it's time to find out exactly which organizations hire people to do the job you want to do. Often you can do the same work in several different organizations or businesses. Your information interviews, along with other research, will help you select the places you most want to work.

> I wish I would have asked more questions about the future of architecture before I decided to become an architect. If I had asked older architects what changes they saw happening to the field, I think could have anticipated some of the frustrations I'm now having with my profession.
>
> —Award-winning architect
> Scott J. Smaby

Building on your information interviews, you will now research more thoroughly the organizations that are likely to offer the job you want. You can research an organization in many ways. Here are just a few of them:

- Look through the archives of newspapers or periodicals and find written information on the organizations.

- Visit their websites.

- Talk to people who work for (or used to work for) organizations you're interested in. Also, talk with competitors (if this is a business) or people at similar agencies (if this is, for example, a nonprofit agency).

- Talk to the suppliers or customers of a business or a particular department of a corporation.

- Ask for information from business leaders in your community, the local chamber of commerce or private industry council, or the state employment office.

When you contact people who work for an organization, or used to work for it, try to figure out the answers to the following questions (some of these are difficult to ask directly; be tactful):

- What kind of work do they do there?

- What are their needs, problems, and challenges?

- What kind of goals are they trying to achieve?

- What obstacles are they running into?

- What kind of reputation do they have within their industry?

- How do they treat their employees?

Also try to find out how your skills and knowledge can help the organization. When you eventually go in for an interview, you want to be able to show that you have something to offer, something that they need. Don't expect your interviewer to make a connection between your past experience and your ability to do this job, even if it's exactly the same work you've done before. You must make your case to the interviewer.

The resources and resource people that you found as you answered the questions above will give you concrete information about potential places of employment as well as a feel for the work environment at each organization you research. Most likely, some will be more appealing to you—and probably a better fit for you—than others. That's exactly what you want to know.

Professional chat rooms and message boards are a great way to network online.

See if you can find people to answer questions about jobs or careers that interest you at **groups.google.com**. Whenever you use the Internet, be sure to observe these basic safety rules:
- Never give out your full name, home address, or phone number.
- If anyone writes anything that creeps you out, cease correspondence and tell an adult you trust about it.

From your research, try to come up with at least five to ten organizations that are potential employers for you. After you've completed your research on various organizations, you will know which ones hire people to do the work you most want to do and which have a work environment that fits you best.

STEP 4: BEGIN YOUR CAMPAIGN TO GET THE JOB YOU WANT

Of the organizations you researched in step 3, choose the top five places you want to work and begin your campaign to get hired. At each of those places, identify the person who has the power to hire you. (This may be the boss in a smaller organization or business, or the hiring manager or a department head in a larger organization.) If you know the name of the person who has the power to hire you, make an appointment. Ask for twenty minutes of his or her time. In asking for an appointment, you can be very direct. Tell this person that you want to discuss the possibility of working for him or her, or with this particular organization or business.

Before your appointment, make an outline of everything you've learned in your information interviewing and your research about this job and company or organization. Be ready to talk about how your skills, training, education, experience, and enthusiasm for this work will make you an outstanding employee.

If there's a company you want to work for and you haven't learned the name of the person who has the power to hire, use your networks—your personal and professional contacts. (Your professional contacts include the people with whom you've done information interviews.) Ask your contacts these questions:

- Do you know someone who works where I want to work?

THE BEST TIME TO CALL . . .

Job hunters have reported that they have great success reaching employers or hiring managers in person at the following times:

- First thing in the morning and last thing in the afternoon.
- Fridays right before and just after lunch

- Can you give me the name of the person who hires for the job I want?

If you can't get an appointment just by calling and asking for one, once again, your network may be able to help. Ask your contacts these questions:

- Do you know the person I want to see?

- Do you know someone who knows the person I want to see?

Ask if your contacts can arrange an introduction for you, or if they can call the person you want to meet and recommend that he or she meet with you.

THE BEST WAYS TO LOOK FOR A JOB

Common Methods	Effectiveness Rate
Using the Internet	4%
Mailing out resumes	7%
Answering ads in trade journals	7%
Answering local want ads*	5–24%
Going to private employment agencies*	5–24%
Asking for job leads from friends and family	33%
Going to see employers, vacancy or not	47%
On your own, using the Yellow Pages to identify employers to contact	69%
Doing the above in a group	84%
Being a job detective**	86%

* The range is due to the level of salary being sought. The higher the salary being sought, the fewer the job hunters who are able to find a job using only this search method.

**A "job detective" follows the strategies used in this book: doing research on oneself, finding jobs that match one's skills and interests, identifying which places of employment have those jobs, and then determining who has the power to hire new staff. We are indebted to parachute trainer Brian McIvor for this concept. The success rate of the job detective method is twelve times higher than if you just send out resumes!

If no offers of employment come from these first five organizations, select five more that have the jobs you want. Keep researching organizations, talking with and expanding the people in your network, and asking for interviews until you receive a job offer.

While you're taking initiative by contacting organizations you'd like to work for, also watch job listings in the newspaper and online. Once you know which organization or business you want to work for, check their website regularly for job listings. If they don't have a website, call their human resources department to find out how you can learn about job openings. Let both your personal and professional networks know that you're looking for work and what type of work you're seeking. The more approaches you use to find your dream job—and the more people who know just what you're looking for—the more likely you'll get that job sooner rather than later.

Job-Search Basics

Now that you know the four steps to searching for and finding the job you want, let's take a closer look at some of the basics that will support and guide you as you take each of those steps.

WHAT YOU NEED FOR YOUR JOB SEARCH

You need to be able to do your job search efficiently in order to be successful. Here are some things you'll need to do that:

- A desk or table.

- Some way of storing, organizing, and retrieving information about yourself, employers, and people you've contacted.

- A secure and reliable way of getting phone messages from employers and other contacts. If you don't have voice mail, invest in it for the length of your job search. Make your outgoing message businesslike. You may also want to mention your job search in your outgoing message. Here's a sample message:

Hi, this is Jessica. I'm sorry I can't take your call right now. Please leave me a message after the beep. I'm currently looking for work in accounting at a hospital or large medical office. If you know of any leads or contacts for me, be sure to mention that too, along with your phone number. Thanks a lot.

- An email address that you can check at least daily. Google, Hotmail, and Yahoo! have free email. Create a businesslike email address. The first initial of your first name with your last name works well. (Many public libraries provide access to the Internet and email for people who don't have a computer.)

- Reliable transportation.

- Appropriate interview clothes. Look at how people are dressed at places you want to work. Wear clothing just a bit more formal than what these workers wear when you go for an information or hiring interview.

HOW TO HAVE A SUCCESSFUL JOB SEARCH

Once you have what you need for your job search, the following techniques and suggestions will help you make that search successful.

SEARCH FULL-TIME

Treat your job search as full-time employment. The more time you spend actively looking for a job, the quicker your job hunt will go. The average job hunter spends only about five hours a week on searching for a job and sees only two employers a week. It's no surprise, then, that the average job search lasts over four months. If you spend more time job searching (using Steps to Your Dream Job, above), you'll find a job much faster.

PROTECT YOUR JOB-SEARCH TIME

Don't let people impose on your job-search time. If you're currently unemployed, your family and friends may be tempted to ask you to do chores or errands. Tell them you'll be glad to help after you finish your job-search activities for the day. Let them know this will be after 3 p.m. If they see that you're serious about devoting at least six hours a day to your job search, they will (hopefully) begin to honor the time you commit to finding the job that's right for you. (And maybe you'll inspire them to find the job that's right for them too!)

MANY VACANCIES AREN'T ADVERTISED

Remember that most vacancies aren't advertised *anywhere*. Research indicates that 75 to 80 percent of open positions are not listed or published. By doing information interviewing and letting people know what type of position you're looking for, you'll be ahead of the game. Of course, you should apply for any advertised vacancy that's of interest to you. Doing that in addition to continuing with your information interviewing and using your network of personal and professional contacts will increase your odds of success.

MAKE LOTS OF PHONE CALLS

Make at least twenty phone calls every morning. Make calls until you've lined up at least two employers who will meet with you each day of the week.

Who do you call? Use the Yellow Pages of your local telephone directory (or a directory from the area where you want to work). Call businesses, companies, agencies, or organizations likely to employ people who do the work you want. Ask for the manager who hires for that work.

What do you say? Create a twenty- to thirty-second pitch. State your name, the work you seek, two or three of your best skills, any machinery or equipment you can operate, or what computer programs you know. Have additional relevant information about your ability to do the job and your prior work experience that you can add in ten- to twenty-second intervals when appropriate in a conversation. You can add the name of your former employer, if you have one or if you think that will make a good impression.

What do you want? Ask for a fifteen-minute appointment to talk further about your potential as an employee. If somebody will see you, go and sell yourself! If there aren't any openings but somebody will see you anyway, go. Use the time to learn more about the business and the state of the industry, as well as to gain practice selling yourself. If there aren't any vacancies and the person doesn't want to see you, ask if he or she knows someone who might be interested in your skills. About 50 percent of the people who use this method have a job in four weeks, and 85 percent have a job in ten weeks.

PRACTICE YOUR PITCH

Write out your pitch and practice it until you can say it slowly and smoothly. Have two or more people listen to it and tell you what they think. Will your pitch get employers interested in seeing you? Here's a good example:

> My name is Shannon O'Neal. I'm looking for warehouse work. I'm very good at driving a forklift, entering shipments into computer programs, and tracking them. I can also receive shipments and figure out how to store them so that they can be easily retrieved in the future. My specialty is preparing shipments so that the driver can make deliveries in an organized and logical manner. I'd like to come in and talk with you about my skills as an employee.

TARGET SMALL ORGANIZATIONS

Begin your job search with organizations that have twenty-five employees or less. If the work you want to do doesn't happen at such a small company, find the smallest company at which it does happen. It's usually easier to find people who hire for small organizations, and easier to get in to see them. Also, small companies can often make faster hiring decisions.

THE ROLE OF LUCK

What is sometimes called "pure dumb luck"—which means having your name in the right place at the right time—plays a crucial role in finding most jobs. But that kind of luck isn't really luck at all but rather the result of good research and savvy networking. The more you meet and talk with people doing the work that you want to do, and the more you keep your professional and personal networks informed about what you're looking for, the more likely you are to get "lucky."

BE PREPARED TO GIVE REFERENCES

If you're looking for a job for the first time, find three or four people (preferably adults who aren't relatives) who will give you references. Employers want to know about your reliability and personality. Have you volunteered at your church or for another nonprofit group? Do you belong to a club? Is there a teacher you like or one in whose class you have worked particularly hard? All of these people have seen you at work (even if it hasn't been paid work) and can comment on their knowledge of you as a student or volunteer worker.

Talk to the people who might provide references for you. Tell them that you're looking for your first paying job, and ask them if they feel they know you or have seen enough of your efforts to give a positive reference. Some will be willing to write you a reference. Others may prefer to give a reference by phone. Try to get at least two or three lined up so that you can provide references quickly if you're asked to do so.

CONSIDER VOLUNTEER WORK

You can do volunteer work while you search for a job, gaining valuable work experience and references in the process. At school, you could volunteer for a leadership program or club. Teachers may be looking for a student assistant, or a peer advising project or tutoring program may need student volunteers. In your community, you might offer to babysit at your church, volunteer at a nonprofit, or even find a local business that would be willing to let you volunteer. See if the organization or agency for which you want to work uses volunteers. If it does, find out how you can become a volunteer there. This is a great way to check out an organization from the inside, and also to get references from people in the organization itself. In order to let your supervisor get to know you, plan on volunteering at least once a week for six weeks to two months.

WHAT—NOTHING ON RESUMES?

You may be starting to wonder why we haven't talked about resumes. This book actually doesn't include anything on resumes for several reasons:

· There are many other places to get help writing a resume (career centers, resume books, career websites).

· Resumes are not a very effective job-search tool, and they're even less effective for younger workers who don't have a great deal of experience in the jobs or fields in which they most want to work.

· Many people depend too much on a resume to get them a job. It's more important to identify your best skills and interests.

If you want to learn more about how and when to use resumes in your job search, please check out this book: *Don't Send a Resume: And Other Contrarian Rules to Help Land a Great Job,* by Jeffrey J. Fox (Hyperion, 2001).

TAKE CARE OF YOURSELF

A job hunt can be very rewarding, but rarely is it easy. It demands physical, mental, and emotional energy. It's important to remember that searching for a job is like anything else—it takes time to do it well, so be gentle with yourself in the job-search process.

Because it's so demanding, a job search can wear down the confidence of even the most positive person. To deal with this, we suggest that you don't focus on whether or not you've gotten the job you want yet. Instead, keep track of how many phone calls, information interviews, hiring interviews, or new contacts you make each day. These numbers mean that you're conducting an effective job search. You also may want to consider creating an "advisory board" for your job search. Arrange to meet once a month with people who are very good at getting jobs they like (perhaps someone you met while doing information interviews), people who know a lot about the industry or field you want to work in, or people who are supportive even when things are challenging. Ask two or three people if you can meet with them once a month to get their advice, suggestions, or simply their support during your job search.

Be sure you take care of your physical needs too. Eat right, get enough sleep, drink eight glasses of water a day, and avoid negative people. Exercise four or five days a week, listen to motivational tapes, see good friends, and watch movies that make you laugh or give you hope. If there are other things you enjoy doing that help you take care of yourself, be sure to incorporate them into your job-search days.

Tips for the Hiring Interview

Hiring interviews can be stressful. They've often been compared to blind dates because people applying for jobs often go interviews without knowing anything about their "date" (the interviewers and the company, organization, or agency where they're interviewing). The more prepared you are, the better your interviews will go. So learn as much as you can about the job you want, the company you want to work for, and which of your skills make you a good candidate for the job. Also study the following tips for before, during, and after the interview. They'll help you make a great impression.

Here are some tips you can you use before, during, and after your interview.

BEFORE YOUR INTERVIEW

Interviewing isn't that hard. It's a matter of knowing how to talk to someone in a focused manner. The more homework you've done on yourself, on the job you want, and on the organization where you have an interview, the better the interview will go.

Before your interview, think about these two basic questions:

1. What do I need to know about this job at this organization?
2. What information do I need to communicate about myself?

To prepare yourself for your interview, practice answering typical interview questions. (See the resources section at the end of this chapter for books and other resources on possible interview questions.) It's helpful to remember that all interview questions are variations on the following questions:

- Why are you here?
- What can you do for us?
- Can I afford you?
- What kind of a person are you? Do I want you to work for me?
- What distinguishes you from nineteen other people who can do the same tasks that you can?

You can think of these as the questions behind the questions. No matter how a question is phrased, if you know what's really being asked, you can choose the best information about yourself to answer the question. Select examples from your experience to show that you've used the skills the job needs, or to show that you pick up new skills quickly. Let's say you're interviewing for a job as a receptionist at a medical office. If you're asked, "What can you do for us?" you might indicate that you've had experience answering phones and taking messages at the insurance office where you worked part-time in high school. As a candy striper, you learned a lot of medical terminology, as well as how to work with people who are ill.

> **THINGS TO AVOID IN AN INTERVIEW**
>
> - Arriving late
> - Bad personal hygiene
> - Excess cologne
> - Inappropriate clothing
> - Lack of initial eye contact
> - Mispronouncing your interviewer's name
> - Rudeness of any sort
> - A weak handshake

Job-search experts report that it takes people about seven interviews to feel comfortable enough to interview well, so do lots of practice interviews. Ask adults or friends you trust to put you through mock interviews. This will help you get better at knowing what to say, how to talk, and when to breathe and think.

DURING YOUR INTERVIEW

Personnel professionals tell us that many interviewers make up their mind about you in the first half-minute of the interview. They spend the remaining time looking for reasons to justify their decision. Here are the three factors that most often influence your interviewer's first impression of you:

1. Were you on time for the interview?
2. Did you look the interviewer in the eye as you greeted him or her?
3. What was the quality of your handshake?

Interviewers also assess your attitude. Here are some things they're likely to notice right away:

TIP: Take a trip to the company or business before your actual interview day. Figure out how long it's likely to take you to get there at the same time of day as your interview. Learn where to park, what bus to take, where the entrance to the building is, and so on. If you do this before the interview, you'll be less stressed the day of the interview. The less stressed-out you are, the more confident you'll seem.

- Whether you're a pleasant person to be around (or not)

- Whether you're interested in other people or totally absorbed with yourself

- If you're at peace with yourself and the world or seething with anger beneath a calm exterior

- If you're outgoing or introverted

- If you're communicative or monosyllabic

- If you're focused on giving or only on taking

- If you're anxious to do the best job possible or just going through the motions

They also notice whether you project energy and enthusiasm or expend only minimal effort and exude a sense of sullenness. In many cases, your attitude is even more important than your skills because it indicates how hard you're willing to work and whether you can work well with other people. Employers will hire someone with lesser skills but with a good attitude before they'll hire a more experienced and more skilled person with a bad attitude.

WHAT INTERVIEWERS NOTICE

A detailed study done by UCLA a couple of years ago revealed some surprising things about what interviewers pay attention to and how much attention they pay to those things.

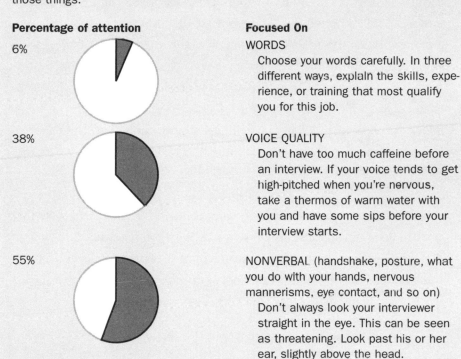

Percentage of attention

6%

38%

55%

Focused On

WORDS
Choose your words carefully. In three different ways, explain the skills, experience, or training that most qualify you for this job.

VOICE QUALITY
Don't have too much caffeine before an interview. If your voice tends to get high-pitched when you're nervous, take a thermos of warm water with you and have some sips before your interview starts.

NONVERBAL (handshake, posture, what you do with your hands, nervous mannerisms, eye contact, and so on)
Don't always look your interviewer straight in the eye. This can be seen as threatening. Look past his or her ear, slightly above the head.

Your interviewer is also trying to judge how quickly you can become productive if you're hired. The way you conduct yourself in the interview gives a lot of clues as to what type of employee you'll be. Here are a few helpful hints for effective interviews:

- Mix speaking and listening equally so the interview feels like a friendly conversation. People hire people they like. If interviewers don't feel comfortable talking with you, they probably won't like you enough to offer you a job.

- Answer the interviewer's questions. Don't go off on tangents. Vary the length of your answers between twenty seconds and two minutes.

- Speak well (or not at all) of your previous employer.

Though it may be hard to believe, remember that many interviewers are as scared as you are during the hiring interview. They don't want to make a hiring mistake. It's definitely to your advantage if you can help make the interviewer feel comfortable. Sometimes it's helpful to remember that *you* are interviewing the interviewer as much as the interviewer is interviewing you—to determine if this is the right job and the right place for you.

In an interview, you're judged just as much on the questions you ask as on those you answer. The questions you ask reveal how much you know about the work, the industry or field, and the organization. Here are two important questions to ask your interviewer.

1. What does this job involve?

You want to understand exactly what tasks will be asked of you so that you can determine if these are the kinds of tasks you really like and want to do. Even if you've done excellent research on this job and employer, you may find that the interviewer has additional or different ideas about what the job will involve. You want to know what those expectations are.

2. What are the skills a top employee in this job needs to have?

You want to know if your skills match those the employer wants a top employee to have. Which of your skills match those of a top employee? Be able to state these skills and give examples of how you've used them in similar situations.

As we said above, you're interviewing the interviewer or employer too. Be sure to ask these three questions of yourself (not the interviewer):

1. **Do I want to work with these people?**

    Pay attention to your intuition. Sometimes your interviewer will give all the "right" answers to your questions, but you'll still have an uneasy feeling. Don't ignore that feeling. You want to know if you can work well with these people and if they share values that are important to you. You want a work environment where you'll thrive. As author and venture capitalist Guy Kawasaki put it, "In a job, your real job is to make your boss look good. During an interview, ask yourself, 'Do I want to make this person look good?'"

2. **Can I do this job? Do I *want* to do this job?**

    Back in chapter 1, we talked about "can-do" skills and "want-to" skills. Be sure you know which skills you really want to use in a job. You're much more likely to be happy in a job that uses a high number of the skills you want to use.

3. **If the job seems to be a good fit, can I persuade the organization that there's something that makes me different from other people who can do the same tasks?**

    It's important to formulate an answer to this question before you walk into the interview. You need to know how you work and be able to describe it. What is the style in which you do your work (for example, independently, collaboratively,

> TIP: You can learn more about writing thank-you notes by doing a search on **www.google.com**. Type "job interview thank-you notes" into the search box.

quickly, carefully, and so on)? Hopefully your style fits with what your hoped-for employer is looking for.

ENDING AN INTERVIEW WITH FINESSE

As the interview proceeds, if the interviewer's questions move from the past toward the future, the interview is going well. If you are *determined* to get a certain job, always ask the five questions below before the end of the interview. Don't be afraid to speak up—you need the answers to these questions.

1. Can you offer me this job? (If you want the job, be sure to ask for it; 20 percent of the people who ask for a job get it.)

2. Do you want me to come back for another interview, perhaps with some of the other decision makers here?

3. When may I expect to hear from you?

4. What is the latest I can expect to hear from you?

5. May I contact you after that date, if for any reason you haven't gotten back to me by that time?

If, however, it's clear from the interview that the interviewer doesn't view you as qualified for this particular job, don't assume all is lost. Be sure to ask these two questions:

1. Do you have work for which you do think I'm qualified?

2. Can you think of anyone else who might be interested hiring me?

TIPS FOR THE HIRING INTERVIEW

Before Your Interview

Ask yourself these questions:

- What information do I need to communicate about myself?

- What do I need to know about this job at this organization?

At Your Interview

- Be on time.

- Look the interviewer in the eye as you greet him or her.

- Shake hands warmly and firmly.

- Ask your interviewer these questions:

—What does this job involve?

—What are the skills a top employee in the job needs to have?

- Ask yourself these questions:

—Do I want to work with these people?

—Can I do this job? Do I *want* to do this job?

—Can I persuade them that there's something that makes me different from other people who can do the same tasks?

After Your Interview

- Always send a thank-you note.

If your faith in finding your dream job is flagging, use your contacts to meet people who have found their dream jobs. Ask them to tell you how they got their job. See if they can help you adapt what they learned to your job search.

Some people get their dream job right away. More people, however, get there in several steps. Each time you have a setback, redouble your efforts to find people doing the work you hope to do, the younger in age the better. If you work at it, you will get there.

Remember, Tony Tallarico had jobs in several levels of the video entertainment industry before taking his current position, where he creates and installs video game arcades. He loves his job. Reread Tony's profile on page 104.

After an Interview

Always send a thank-you note to your interviewer. If more than one person was involved in the interview, send a thank-you note to each person on the interview team. (To review thank-you note basics, see chapter 4.)

- Thank your interviewer for his or her time.

- If you enjoyed meeting the interviewer, say so.

- Remind the interviewer of one or two parts of your background (skills, training, or previous jobs) that qualify you for the job. When you write your note, don't make it too long. A letter of just three or four paragraphs (with three to four sentences in each paragraph) can be read quickly. A longer letter may make

SAMPLE THANK-YOU NOTE

(Date)
Dear Mr. Monroe:

Thank you so much for interviewing me for the job of nurse's aide. I was so impressed that you took the time to show me around and introduce me to some of the other employees.

I feel my training makes me very qualified for this job. My experience helping my grandmother after her last surgery taught me how to work with older patients who are sick or slightly confused.

I hope I'll hear from you on Friday, as you indicated. If not, I'll call you next week.

Sincerely,
Sean Jones

your interviewer think that you're doing another interview in writing rather than saying thank you. Always make certain your note— whether typed or email—is grammatically correct with no spelling errors. Send it within twenty-four hours of your interview.

You're Hired! Now What?

Congratulations! All your hard work has paid off and you've been hired. Enjoy the good news and be sure to celebrate.

Now, of course, you'll start your new job. Is there something else you should be doing? John Crystal, author and creative job-search pioneer, once said, "To take charge of your career, you need to look further down the road than headlight range. You need to begin your next job hunt the day you start your current job."

Ugh! That's probably not what you wanted to hear. But taking charge of your career is simply a continuation of what you've already been doing— from identifying your skills and interests to naming your potential dream jobs, from getting the appropriate training or education to researching and interviewing for this particular job. It may be that the job you've just gotten isn't quite your dream job, but it is a step on the way toward that dream job. To help you continue on the road to your dream job, we have a few more recommendations for you.

START A JOB JOURNAL

Each week, spend ten to fifteen minutes making notes about what you did during the week. Jot down names of projects, tasks, activities, or important meetings. Make notes about what should be included in a future job portfolio. Note what you like with + and use − for job duties you didn't like. Be sure to include committees you've been asked to serve on, and the names of professional organizations you've joined. (Also note any offices you may hold.)

It's easy to forget all the tasks and responsibilities of a job. Write them down so you won't forget. Your job journal will be a valuable resource when you face performance reviews and self-evaluations, as well as when you begin the search for your next job or take the next step toward your dream job.

IDENTIFY THE MEMBERS OF THE "A TEAM"

As you become familiar with your new work environment, note the people throughout the organization. Who are the up-and-comers? Is there a manager you would rather work for or a division you would rather work in? Get to know the people who have the jobs you want. Get to know their managers too. Don't go around saying, "I want your job"; you won't build good relations with your colleagues that way. But do ask people about the specifics of their job. By doing information interviews at work, you can develop a plan for the next step in your career.

WATCH, LISTEN, AND LEARN

If you join a business, division, or department that has two or more people, be aware that you're entering a situation that has a history. There are ongoing dynamics and power struggles about which you know nothing. As you begin to learn your way around, observe everyone and everything. After a few weeks of watching the scene, you'll probably put together what's going on.

FIND A MENTOR

If this is an industry or company in which you hope to have a long-term career, find a mentor. (For more on mentors, see chapter 5.) This person may work for the same company you do, work elsewhere, or be retired. Choose someone who has achieved the level of success to which you aspire.

• • • • •

We've covered a lot of important territory in this chapter. We hope you've learned a lot about how to search for and find your dream job. In the next chapter, we'll look at the top ten mistakes job-hunters make—and how *you* can avoid them.

If You Want to Explore Further . . .

JOB HUNTING: GENERAL INFORMATION

Bermont, Todd. *10 Insider Secrets to a Winning Job Search: Everything You Need to Get the Job You Want in 24 Hours—or Less.* Career Press, 2004.

Coon, Nora. *Teen Dream Jobs: How to Find the Job You Really Want Now!* Beyond Words Publishing, 2003.

Covey, Sean. *The 7 Habits of Highly Effective Teens.* Fireside, 1998.

Culbreath, Alice, and Saundra Neal. *Testing the Waters: A Teen's Guide to Career Exploration.* JRC Consulting, 1999.

Edwards, Mark. *The Famous Outrageous Cool Kid's Guide to the Future: The Unique Career Guide for Pre-Teens and Young Teens Based on Their Talents and Interests.* Medwards, 1999.

Figler, Howard. *The Complete Job Search Handbook.* Henry Holt Publishers, 1999.

Fox, Jeffrey J. *Don't Send a Resume: And Other Contrarian Rules to Help Land a Great Job.* Hyperion, 2001.

Webster, Jeanne. *If You Could Be Anything, What Would You Be? A Teen's Guide to Mapping Out the Future.* Dupuis North Publishing, 2004.

This fun site has career advice and job listings for the upper Midwest states:

www.jobdig.com/

This site has job listings around the country and around the world:

www.craigslist.org/

For links to Internet employment resources, check out:

www.jobhunt.com/

JOB HUNTING: INTERVIEW PREPARATION

Gottesman, Deb, and Buzz Mauro. *The Interview Rehearsal Book.* Berkley Trade, 1999.

Kador, John. *201 Best Questions to Ask on Your Interview.* McGraw-Hill, 2002.

Porot, Daniel, and Frances Haynes. *The 101 Toughest Interview Questions.* Ten Speed Press, 1999.

JOB HUNTING: SPECIAL RESOURCES

Bolles, Richard Nelson, and Dale S. Brown. *Job-Hunting for the So-Called Handicapped*. Ten Speed Press, 2001. This book deals with the specific challenges faced by job hunters with disabilities.

Kruempelmann, Elizabeth. *The Global Citizen: A Guide to Creating an International Life and Career.* Ten Speed Press, 2002. As the title suggests, this is geared toward people who want to work and experience life abroad.

Landes, Michael. *The Back Door Guide to Short-Term Job Adventures*, 4th edition. Ten Speed Press, 2005. This book includes loads of great information on internships, seasonal work, volunteer jobs, and adventures abroad.

MENTORING

This site has general information about mentoring. Enter your zip code to find programs in your area.

www.mentoring.org/

NEW JOBS—AFTER YOU'RE HIRED

Williams, Anna, et al. *The Family Guide to the American Workplace.* Learnovation, 2003. See especially chapters 3 (Beginning Your New Job) and 4 (Learning the Job).

This fun companion website to Bob Rosner's book *Working Wounded* (Warner Books, 2000) offers solutions to common workplace problems:

www.workingwounded.com/

SALARY INFORMATION

Some job descriptions give salary information based on national averages. The area where you want to live may have salaries higher or lower than the national norm. To check out salaries by zip code, check out this website:

www.salary.com/

the top 10 mistakes job hunters make—and how YOU can avoid them

Along with the job-search strategies and techniques you're learned in the previous chapters, avoiding the mistakes job hunters commonly make will put you ahead in the job-hunting game. Here are the ten most common mistakes and how you can avoid them.

1. ACTING AS IF SOMEONE OWES YOU A JOB

Successful job hunters don't feel an employer owes them a job, but they do make every effort to let the employer know that they would be an excellent employee, thus impressing the employer with their enthusiasm and attitude. In the job-search process, it's important to remember that no one owes you a job. If you want a particular job, put all your effort into going after it and use everything that you've learned about yourself and how to be an effective job hunter.

2. SPENDING TOO LITTLE TIME ON THE JOB SEARCH

Successful job hunters quickly learn that the amount of success they experience in their job hunt is in direct proportion to their job-hunting effort. Two-thirds of all job hunters spend five hours or less a week on their job search. Let's say you know it will take you 150 hours to get a new job. If you put in six hours a day, five days a week, you'd find a job in five weeks. If you job hunt one hour a day, five days a week, it will take you thirty weeks (seven and a half months) to find a job. Which approach seems best to you?

> What accounts for the difference between greatness and mediocrity? Extraordinary drive.
> —Benjamin Bloom

Obviously, it's not possible to know exactly how long it will take you to find a job because the job hunt is full of factors you can't predict or control. But one thing's for sure: the more hours you put into your job hunt, the more likely it is that you'll find a job you really want, especially if you use the job-search techniques explained in this book. If you aren't getting the results you want in your job search, increase the amount of time you spend job hunting each day until you get the results you want.

3. CONTINUING TO USE TECHNIQUES THAT AREN'T WORKING

Successful job hunters change tactics when change is needed. When any job-hunting behavior, attitude, or technique doesn't work for you, try something new. (See chapter 8 for specific tactics to use.) For example, if you haven't had any interviews after a month of using a certain technique—say, sending out resumes or answering ads—change your tactics. Start doing more information interviews and spend more time researching organizations that you find interesting.

I received an email from someone whose most recent job was in microelectronics. He wanted another job in that industry. It took him fourteen hundred inquiries to get the message that the semiconductor industry in the U.S. is dead—it has almost completely been moved to Asia. If you make ten inquiries and everyone says no one's hiring, expand your geographic boundaries, or change your target field.

—Marty Nemko, career coach and author of *Cool Careers for Dummies*

Expand what you've learned in this book about effective job-search techniques by reading other good job-search books and consulting online resources. (See the resources sections at the end of preceding chapters.) Talk with successful job hunters and ask what worked for them. Find a support group for job hunters. Your local employment office may sponsor one; some churches do, as well.

4. IGNORING WHAT OTHERS HAVE LEARNED

People who succeed in job hunting talk with other successful job hunters. As we suggested in #3, above, it's important to talk with people who have succeeded in finding a job they love. Learn from people who are job-hunting masters.

Ask family members, friends, teachers, and others in your personal and professional networks to help you find successful job hunters. Talk to at least four people who have found a job that they like in the last six months. Use every technique that worked for them. If necessary, modify the techniques to fit the job you seek.

Job-search mentors can also be very helpful. You need more than one person's point of view for good perspective, so ask two to four people to mentor you through your job hunt. If you know some people who you think are pretty sharp, ask them if they'd be willing to meet with you once a month to advise you. Each time you meet, update them on what you've done and for ask for their ideas on how to improve.

5. PLAYING AT JOB HUNTING

Successful job hunters treat the job hunt as a job, not as a game. Think of yourself as having a full-time job (without pay) from 9 a.m. to 5 p.m. every weekday. By 9 a.m. each weekday, be showered, groomed, and dressed in business casual. If you aren't sure how to dress, visit the places you want to work and see how people are dressed. Then select clothing one notch more formal. If you're dressed for work, you can be out the door quickly if someone says, "I can see you now." Job hunters who have great success at getting hiring interviews report that they spend five to eight hours a day in job-search activities such as creating an overall job-search strategy, reviewing skills and experience relevant to the work desired, identifying job targets, making contacts, reading articles on job-search techniques, doing Internet research, setting up interviews, and writing thank-you notes.

6. BEING FINANCIALLY UNPREPARED

Successful job hunters assess their financial situation realistically—unsuccessful job hunters don't. Most likely, your job search will last between two and eighteen weeks, even if you work at it full-time. Prepare yourself mentally and financially for your job hunt. Assume it will last a lot longer than you think it will. Ask yourself these questions:

- Given the money in my pocket, bank account, savings, piggy bank, or other sources, how long can I afford to live without having a job?

- Can I get help with buying interview clothes or paying for transportation costs and Internet access?

- Am I eligible for any assistance from public agencies or nonprofit organizations in my area?

- Am I living at home or can I move back home?

- What support can my parents provide? (Ask how long they're willing to support you while you look for a job. Don't assume their financial support will go on indefinitely.)

- Can I lower my expenses? (Thoroughly assess your financial resources and put the brakes on unnecessary spending.)

- Can I move to a less expensive place?

- Can I earn part of my rent in exchange for doing chores or maintenance?

7. GIVING UP TOO EASILY AND TOO SOON

> The one thing a job-hunter needs above everything else is hope, and hope is born of persistence.
>
> —Richard N. Bolles, author of *What Color Is Your Parachute?*

Successful job hunters are persistent. Various studies on job hunting indicate that one-third of all job hunters *give up* during the first two months of their job hunt. They give up because they thought job hunting would be simple, quick, and easy. (In times when the nation's economy isn't doing well, job-search experts estimate that job hunters need to make about two hundred contacts before finding a job.)

Many employers eliminate job hunters from consideration for jobs on the grounds of their job-search behavior, especially any lack of initiative and persistence, so keep going until you find a job. Here are some examples of being persistent:

- Sending an email resume, then sending a resume by mail, then following up a few days later with a phone call

- Being willing to go back to places that interest you to see if by any chance their "no vacancy" or interest in you has changed

- Asking yourself, "What businesses need someone with my skills?" until you find one that wants to hire you

- Making the fourth, fifth, or sixth phone call to find someone who knows the people who have the power to hire at the places you want to work

8. HAVING ONLY ONE JOB TARGET

Successful job hunters have more than one job target. They are well aware that in this rapidly changing world, jobs do vanish. Therefore, using your interests, experience, values, best skills, and whatever else is important to you in a job, identify three or four other lines of work you can do, and would enjoy doing. Never put all your eggs in one basket.

Be open to new possibilities. Don't label yourself so that you think there's only one thing you can do. Don't define yourself in terms of your current or former job title. You are not a fast-food worker, a retail salesperson, or an army vet. Define yourself in terms of the *skills* you have.

Ironically, defining yourself—and your job hunt—too broadly can be just as detrimental as defining yourself and the job you're looking for too narrowly. Don't tell others you're looking for "anything." Be specific about the jobs you want and look for.

9. LIMITING YOUR JOB SEARCH TO WHAT'S "OUT THERE"

Successful job hunters go after the jobs they want the most, even if those jobs aren't advertised. You can do that too. Remember, you'll be more likely to find something you want if you look for something you want. (Review Steps to Your Dream Job in chapter 8.)

10. THINKING YOU MUST DO THIS ALL BY YOURSELF

Successful job hunters ask for help. Once you know what kind of work you're looking for, get out your address book or PDA. Call everyone you know. Tell them what work you want and ask if they know someone who does that work. If you know where you want to work, ask them if they know someone who works at that place. Ask your parents, relatives, friends, friends' parents, teachers, people you know at your place of worship, and current or former coworkers for suggestions of other people you might contact. Follow up on every lead you are given.

The most effective—and least used—strategy is to meet at least twelve people who either do exactly the work you want to do or are employed in the same industry. Ask them to notify you if they hear of job openings that fit what you're looking for. These twelve people then become twelve more pairs of eyes and ears helping you with your job search.

TIP: Find a job-search buddy. Do you (or anyone in your personal or professional network) know of someone who is looking for work? You'll be more persistent, get more support, uncover more leads, and even have more fun if you job hunt with a friend.

• • • • •

By avoiding these top ten mistakes, you will become a successful job hunter. When you need a quick review of job-search basics, come back to this list. Knowing what *not* to do—and even more importantly, knowing what *to do*—will put you way ahead of less determined job hunters.

beyond your dream job

CREATING THE LIFE YOU WANT

You've probably heard the saying "There's more to life than work." We agree wholeheartedly with that saying and would add that there's even more to life than the very good and fulfilling work that we hope you'll find in your dream job. Though our main focus here has been to prepare you to find that dream job, we have an even deeper purpose for writing this book. That purpose is to help you live a good and fulfilling life—to live your *whole* life.

> The power of vision is extraordinary.
>
> —DeWitt Jones, award-winning *National Geographic* photographer

In this chapter, we invite you to explore what that whole life means for you. We'll begin by asking you to reflect on the people, things, and activities that you want to include in your life. Next, we'll ask you to delve a bit deeper and consider the underpinnings of your life—your values and beliefs, what we call your "philosophy of life." After that, we encourage you to look at those people you respect and admire—your role models—and consider how they can help you become the person you want to be. Finally, we'll invite you to look at your purpose or mission in life—what it is that you've been put on earth to do and who you are to be. In each of these areas, we'll ask you to spend time reflecting on different aspects of your life—how you want to live your life and what type of person you most want to be. Only you can answer those questions.

Envisioning Your Life, Defining Your Future

What kind of life do you want? Knowing what you want is the first step to making that life happen. We've spent a lot of time discovering what it is you want in your dream job. But what else do you want? How do you want to fill your hours outside of work? What about being alive is most important to you? Here are a few things you might want as part of your whole life:

- Friends, family, a life partner, children, pets

- Sports and outdoor activities

- Cultural activities (theater, music, dance)

- Travel and time for hobbies

- Involvement with community or religious organizations

- Participation in political or environmental causes

Obviously, there are many more things you can do with your time outside work, but hopefully those given above will be enough to get you thinking about what you want in your life. Another way of looking at it is to think about what you enjoy doing now and want to continue doing. Also consider whether anything is missing from your life that you want to be a part of your future.

For example, what kind of family life do you want to have as an adult, particularly in relation to your work? Will it be like the family life you have now, or will it be different? Kyle, age fifteen, wants something different because, as he puts it, "My dad hides out at work." Family life is often neglected these days. Parents spend 40 percent less time with their children in 2005 than they did in 1960. If you want to have children, what kind of parent do you want to be? What kind of family life do you want to have?

Lisa, age fifteen, also wants something different because, she says, "Sometimes adults make it seem like all they do is work. This doesn't make being an adult very attractive." What would make being an adult attractive to you? Which adults do you admire—and why?

The following exercise will help you envision your future and the way you want to live your life, including what and who you want to play a part in it. Pretend a magic wand has been waved over your life, giving you everything that's important to you in your ideal life. Have fun with this, but also give yourself plenty of time to think about what matters most to you. You might want to complete this exercise over several days or even a few weeks to let what's really important to you rise to the surface. The goal is to have a visual image—a concrete vision—of your ideal life.

> Don't confuse life and work. It is much easier to write a resume than to craft a spirit.
>
> —Anna Quindlen, writer

Picturing Your Ideal Life

To do this exercise, you'll need the following materials:

- A large piece of white paper
- Colored pencils or pens
- Old magazines that you can cut up
- Scissors
- Glue

(If you have computer skills for doing graphic art, you may prefer to use your computer for this exercise.)

Draw pictures or symbols, or create a collage to express visually the kind of life you want to live. Use the questions below to get yourself thinking about what you want to include in your picture (but be sure to add anything else that's important to you):

- In your ideal life, where do you live (city, suburb, rural area, on an island, in the mountains)?
- What kind of house or living space do you want?
- What is your neighborhood like?
- Who is with you (friends, family, pets)?
- What you do for a living?
- Do you want to travel? Where do you want to go?
- Where do you want to vacation?
- What activities—sports, cultural, religious/spiritual, family, community—do you want to participate in?

You may want to work on your picture for several days until you feel it truly represents the life you want.

Now, look at your picture again. Take a few minutes to think about what you need to do to help make this ideal life happen. Because you can't do everything at once, choose one area that you can do something about now. (You may want to return to chapter 7 to review how to set short-term and long-term goals.) Having a vision of what you want your life to be is an important step in helping it become reality.

Once you have a concrete vision of your future, let's explore more deeply how you want to live that life and who you want to be. This includes discovering the unique contribution you have to make to the world and finding meaning in life—in your individual life and in the world around you. As you live, love, and learn more about life, you'll create—spoken or unspoken—a philosophy of life, a way in which you understand and view life events and people. A philosophy of life also helps you to interpret and understand your life experiences. For some, this meaning will be grounded in their religious or spiritual beliefs and the interaction of those beliefs with their life experiences; for others, it will grow more directly out of their life experiences. We invite you to take a few minutes now to reflect on your philosophy of life.

Writing Your Philosophy of Life

Everyone needs an "operating manual" for his or her life. That's really what a philosophy of life is. It identifies what you value most in life and articulates how you want to live your life. Your life philosophy will also guide your decisions.

Begin by writing down what is most important to you (for example, family, friends, money, art, freedom, or whatever). Think about why these are important to you and why you want them to be a part of your life. You may find that this exercise overlaps some with the previous exercise—friends and family, for example, may come up in both exercises. That's fine. Now, go a bit further and think about particular qualities that are important to you, such as truth, integrity, peace, compassion, or forgiveness.

Next, list the beliefs by which you intend to live your life (for example, all people are created equal, creation is sacred, or love is more powerful than hate). Then think about how you'll face difficult times in your life. How do you hope you'll react to obstacles that may block the path to your goals? How will you deal with loss or frustration?

Give yourself time to think about what you value and believe. Think about what makes your life meaningful. Work on your philosophy of life for ten minutes a day for a week, or spend some time on it each weekend for a month or two. See what emerges as you reflect on these important matters. Your philosophy of life will evolve and grow as you do. Revisit the questions above from time to time to think about what matters most to you.

If you hit a rough patch in life, reviewing your philosophy of life will help you assess what went wrong and how to get back on track. If you're ever disappointed with yourself or your life, ask yourself these questions:

· Am I paying attention to what I value most?
· Am I living my life by what I most deeply believe?

Your philosophy of life shapes everything that you do, as well as everything you are and are becoming. It shapes all aspects of your life. Just as you created a concrete vision of your future life in the discovery exercise Picturing Your Ideal Life, writing out your philosophy of life will help you articulate how you want to live your life. And, as we said before, knowing what you want is the first step to making it happen.

Becoming the Person You Want to Be

As you picture your ideal life and articulate your philosophy of life, you may also want to reflect on what kind of person you want to be. When you think about the person you want to be, you'll undoubtedly think about people who are important to you—people who have helped, inspired, befriended, or supported you through thick and thin. Who are the people you respect and admire? Who are your role models? Take a few moments now to reflect on those people, who, by their lives and example, can help you become the person you want to be.

> Those who preserve their integrity remain unshaken by the storms of daily life. They do not stir like leaves on a tree or follow the herd where it runs. In their mind remains the ideal attitude and conduct of living. This is not something given to them by others. It is their roots. . . . It is a strength that exists deep within them.
>
> —Anonymous Native American

Reflecting on the traits you value—those that you most admire in the people you consider to be your role models—can help you cultivate those traits in your own life. If you can, arrange to talk with one or more of your role models about a trait of theirs that you particularly admire, for example, their compassion, intellect, wit, honesty, or ability to make people feel comfortable. Ask them how they developed that trait and who their role models were and are. See if they have suggestions as to how you can develop that trait in your own life.

My Role Models

Take a sheet of paper and turn it so that the long edge is horizontal. Fold the sheet in half, crease it, and then fold it in half again. You should have four columns of equal width.

At the top of the first column (starting at the left), write "Names of people I admire." Under that heading, make a list of people you admire. These can be real people you know or have known, historical figures, or fictional characters from books, movies, comic books, or TV.

At the top of the second column, write "What I admire about them or their lives." Think about each person in the first column, and then write down what you admire about them.

At the top of the third column, write "Do I have this trait?" Read over the traits you've written for each of the people you admire. Ask yourself, "Do I have this trait? Do I want to have this trait?" Write your answers in the third column.

At the top of the last column, write "How can I develop this trait?" Answer this question for each trait or attribute you'd like to develop or strengthen.

Discovering Your Mission in Life

You've been reflecting on very important aspects of your life—how you want to live your life, what you most deeply value and believe, and who you most deeply admire. Your reflections on these questions, along with the other explorations you've made in this book, will help find your purpose or mission in life—that is, what you are alive to do. Each of us has a purpose for being alive, and through our mission, we use our unique talents to contribute something to the world, making it a better place to live, both for us now and for the generations that will follow us. There are three aspects to this mission:

1. Our lives are not simply to be filled with *doing* things; who we are and how we live our lives—our very *being*—is also important.

2. We are to do what we can do—moment by moment, day by day—to make this world a better place. In every situation, we each must do

what we can to bring more gratitude, kindness, forgiveness, honesty, and love into the world.

3. Each of us must discover our purpose in life—how to use the talent that we came to earth to use. To do this, we each need to find and use our greatest gift—the gift that delights us when we use it—in the places or with the people where we are drawn to use that gift and where it is most needed in the world.

As you seek your mission in life, always remember that you have something important to offer the world. The gift you are and the gift you have to offer are unique. Only *you* can be you. Only you can fulfill your mission. Only you can give your unique gift to make the world a better place.

Our Wish for You

As we close, we wish you well as you discover yourself, define your future, and live out your mission in life. May you find work that challenges, satisfies, and delights you. May that work be part of a whole life that is good and fulfilling in every way. May you live out your life purpose, your mission, and give what only you can give to make the world a better place.

Be careful. Be thorough. Be persistent. Live fully, love deeply, and always remember that step by step, day by day, you are creating your life and your future. May it be glorious!

Appendix

MORE INFORMATION INTERVIEWS

ACTRESS

NAME: Tyler Gannon   **AGE:** 20

JOB TITLE: Actress/model

FIELD(S): Film/entertainment industries

EMPLOYER: Self

DEGREE: None

TRAINING: Ongoing since age five

COST OF TRAINING: $2,000–4,000 per year

SALARY: SAG (Screen Actor's Guild) union scale is about $547 a day. Commercials can earn residuals, or are offered as "buyouts, which is a bit more money than scale, but no residuals. A large national commercial can earn you $5,000–30,000. There are different rates for speaking and nonspeaking roles.

You're allowed to work once without having to join the union. Then you have to join SAG. I got my SAG card at age six. It cost $900 then, but it's gone up considerably. The companion union that covers TV and radio is AFTRA (American Federation of Television and Radio Artists). You have to join both unions, and never let your dues lapse!

SALARY WITH THREE TO SIX YEARS EXPERIENCE: An actor could still be making scale, or if you're specifically requested for a role, it could be double or even triple scale. Your agent takes 10 percent of your gross pay. Or, you could be unemployed and waiting tables while looking for your next job.

WHAT DO YOU DO?

My main focus is motion-picture acting. I've had roles in two Lifetime Network films, and I've been in several independent film projects. Last year I completed my first lead role in a film called *Film Geek* by Portland filmmaker James Westby. I also had a role in the movie *Thumbsucker* by Mike Mills. That film premiered at this year's Sundance Film Festival in the feature competition.

I've also been in TV commercials for AT&T, Toyota, and Mattel. I've done print modeling for Hanna, Andersen, Nike, and Espirit and some radio voice-over work as well.

HOW LONG HAVE YOU BEEN DOING THIS WORK?

I've been working since I was five. Fifteen years of my life have already been dedicated to studying and working. It hasn't been a solid, steady stream of work. It seems like when you're working, you might have a few projects going at once, and then nothing for six months. This can be excruciating and discouraging to people who are just starting out, but if this is your passion, nothing compares to when you do get to work and get paid for doing what you love to do.

HOW DID YOU GET INTO THIS WORK?

I've known this was what I wanted to do my entire life. When I was five, I remember watching a Barbie commercial on Saturday morning and asking my parents, "Can I do that?" Their answer was, "Do you want to do that?" And, of course, the answer was yes.

Being a child actor, I spent almost every day in the backseat of a car on my way to an audition.

WHAT DO YOU LIKE ABOUT YOUR JOB?

When you actually do get to work, there is nothing more rewarding! Being a part of a cast and crew is really a unique experience. The whole time you'll be asking yourself, "Am I really getting paid for this?" Developing another character, living and seeing through their eyes, and being truthful through their point of view is a feeling that is beyond comparison.

WHAT DON'T YOU LIKE ABOUT YOUR JOB?

I hate that there isn't steady work. I dislike that there are a lot of people who want to take advantage of your naïveté. That's another reason it's so important to take acting classes from teachers with good reputations within the acting world. You hear important information (*not* gossip).

I never tell anyone my personal views about other people in the business, however close I think I am to them. This industry is like high school, rumors fly and it can make you look extremely unprofessional.

WHAT ARE THE MAIN CHALLENGES IN THIS INDUSTRY?

Phonies, users, time wasters, drugs, alcohol, and, most important, keeping your integrity.

WHAT DO YOU SEE HAPPENING IN THIS FIELD IN THE NEXT FIVE TO TEN YEARS?

There will mostly be amazing things happening technology-wise. Digital video means it's completely possible to shoot your own high-quality independent projects, and there is an established circuit of independent film festivals where those works can be screened and purchased for distribution by the established studios. A great story is a great story, and you can convey that story effectively on a shoestring budget these days, and it looks great. It doesn't have to be a hundred-million-dollar project.

Some people are worried about rendered characters replacing real actors. I don't perceive that as a threat because rendered characters have been around since Mickey Mouse. They can coexist. There is something about true human emotion and interaction that cannot be duplicated or replaced. I truly believe there will always be a need for actors.

WHAT IS YOUR ULTIMATE CAREER GOAL?

I would love to make a substantial living at what I do, but only a small percentage of actors achieve that. I would be happy continuing to do small projects the rest of my life, as long as I got to act. I will continue to work on my skills and better myself as an actor. Creation is an ongoing process. I will always act, if not for a living, then just because I love doing it.

TYLER'S ADDITIONAL COMMENTS

My parents helped me find great representation. The younger you jump into this industry the better. There are still a lot of unspoken rules that nobody is going to tell you. There's not a handbook to look at or an etiquette sheet to refer to; everyone has to learn these things through experience. That really is the most difficult part. Just like so many other things in life, if it were easy, everyone would do it. You must stay confident and refuse to be typecast. That's hard when you're just one of the many in the sea of newbies. You must remind yourself you are one of a kind, and always remember you can offer things that no one else can.

P R O F I L E

NAME: Peter Kelly **AGE:** 29

JOB TITLE: Computer animator

FIELD(S): Special effects/entertainment

EMPLOYER: Industrial Light and Magic

DEGREE(S): BA, liberal arts, St. Mary's College; BA, art, California Institute of the Arts

STUDENT LOANS: $28,000

MONTHLY PAYMENT: $240

SALARY: Starting: $44,375–49,575; three to six years experience: $51,000–67,000*

*Salary info from salary.com

WHAT DO YOU DO?

It is my job to create a specified performance for a computer-generated character in a motion picture. I use the computers and software here at work as my tools to get that performance the way the director wants it in the film. The characters that we use are like puppets in our computers, and we can manipulate their bodies to create that performance. I can also control all the details in a character's face to create emotion, eye blinks, and any other traits that would help to bring that character to life.

DO YOU SUPERVISE ANYONE?

I don't supervise anyone here right now. I am helping to mentor a production assistant who wants to learn more about animation, but that is for his own growth and isn't related to a production.

HOW LONG HAVE YOU BEEN IN THIS JOB?

I've been a computer animator here at Industrial Light and Magic for three and a half years.

WHAT DO YOU LIKE ABOUT YOUR JOB?

I have to say that I love my job and I find myself very lucky to be working on some amazing projects like *The Hulk* and episodes 2 and 3 of *Star Wars.*

WHAT DON'T YOU LIKE ABOUT YOUR JOB?

One thing that I sometimes don't like is that I'm usually trying to get my animation to look perfect for another director or supervisor. Sometimes it's frustrating when the director wants a change that I don't agree with, or when I have to change some animation that I like to get it finaled and in the movie. But it's my job to get that performance right for the director and not for me.

WHAT DO YOU SEE HAPPENING IN THIS FIELD IN THE NEXT FIVE TO TEN YEARS?

I certainly see the opportunity for more advanced computer-generated characters in movies. But I also think we are going to be using more of a technique called "motion capture." Motion capture (or mo-cap for short) is when you have an actor act out a scene while wearing a special suit that records all of his or her motion into the computer.

An animator then takes that data and makes all the necessary changes to get the scene finaled without creating the scenes themselves. There are still some challenging aspects to motion capture, but it isn't as fun and fulfilling as regular computer animation.

WHAT IS YOUR ULTIMATE CAREER GOAL?

I would love to sit in a theater and watch as an audience reacts to my animation up on the screen. I have worked on some great opportunities, but I'm still a little too new or "green" to get those monumental shots in our movies. Someday I also want to be a lead animator, in charge of a crew, and oversee a project.

OTHER INTERESTS

I enjoy running, biking, and swimming when I'm not working. I was very active with my triathlon training until my Ironman last July. I try to draw and play my guitar as much as possible.

PETE'S ADDITIONAL COMMENTS

If you were to tell me four years ago that I would now be a computer animator at ILM, I would never have believed you. Back then I loved the traditional method of drawing and flipping many drawings to create a performance. I was inspired by the old Disney animated classics. I even studied traditional animation at California Institute of the Arts for three years.

The folks at ILM saw some of my work from CalArts and hired me into a training or apprentice position, where I learned how to take what I knew as a traditional animator and apply it to the computer world. Currently, there isn't much work out there for the traditional animators and everyone is learning computer animation.

Now, I would prefer to work on a computer over the old drawing method that I used to love. I guess you never know where your career will take you.

P R O F I L E

MEDICAL DOCTOR

NAME: Serena Brewer   AGE: 29

JOB TITLE: Medical resident

FIELD(S): Family practice medicine

EMPLOYER: The National Health Service Corps

DEGREE: Doctor of osteopathic medicine

TRAINING: Four years of medical school plus three years of residency

COST: $240,000

SALARY: $36,000–41,000 (during residency); $60,000+ (after residency)

WHAT DO YOU DO?

I'm a first-year resident in a three-year family practice residency program that will train me to be a family physician.

ACTIVITIES

I spend seventy to eighty hours a week providing patient care in family practice clinic. This involves anything from checkups to stitches to prenatal visits. Beyond that, my activities change with my schedule each month—some months my activities center around delivering babies, other months around admitting people to a hospital when they're sick or injured, and others around surgery.

WHAT DO YOU LIKE ABOUT YOUR JOB?

I love that every day brings multiple new challenges to my skills and learning thus far, as well as opportunities to teach people about both how their bodies function and how to take care of them.

WHAT DON'T YOU LIKE ABOUT YOUR JOB?

More and more, to have a successful medical practice requires business skills and training, which you don't get in medical school. I don't like that I spend almost as much time each day wading through paperwork and negotiating with insurance companies as I do helping patients.

HOW LONG HAVE YOU BEEN IN THIS JOB?

This is my first year as a resident. I'll spend a total of three years training in family practice before moving to a rural community for four years as a service repayment to the program that funded my medical training.

WHAT IS YOUR ULTIMATE CAREER GOAL?

To own my own small family practice in the Pacific Northwest that can provide health care to the insured and uninsured alike.

WHAT DO YOU SEE HAPPENING IN THIS FIELD IN THE NEXT FIVE TO TEN YEARS?

A major shortage in both primary and specialized care providers. Unless the current insurance laws are reformed, fewer and fewer physicians will be able to afford the costs of maintaining a medical practice. Those physicians who choose to brave it out will find themselves with increasing patient burdens and increasing financial obligations that will likely be passed on to the patient as higher and higher costs of care. On the plus side, the shortage will widen the recruiting pool for future physicians.

SERENA'S ADDITIONAL COMMENTS

My career path started in high school with a notion that I wanted to help people, particularly with physical activities. I looked initially at physical therapy; however, I quickly realized it was the physician who sent someone to physical therapy who ultimately had the most control over a patient's recovery.

So down the path I went, exploring medical school and physical and rehabilitative medicine. In college, I grew increasingly aware that the traditional medical school approach wasn't for me. By graduation, I hadn't made up my mind, so I took a few years off to work in the "real world." On the side, I kept up my interests in the human body and healing by training in massage therapy.

Through massage therapy contacts, I was introduced to osteopathic medicine, which believes in treating the whole person rather than just a specific issue or injury. I knew instantly this was the approach to medicine and healing that best fit me. (In retrospect, most of my MD colleagues have an almost identical approach to those of us who are DOs, but at the time, when I had to choose where to train, I felt most at home in osteopathic programs.)

At the same time, my interest in rehabilitative medicine gradually gave way to an interest in teaching people how to care for their bodies and stay healthy, especially people with limited income. So once again my goals shifted—from rehabilitative medicine to family medicine. In medical school, there were very few specialties that I didn't enjoy, but time and time again, what I loved most was working in the family practice clinics and the wider variety of health issues I encountered there every day.

If you think you're at all interested in a career in health care, find someone who does what you're interested in and spend the day with them. Ask them how they got to where they are. Most of us in health care would love to share our stories and make it easier for those who come after us. And definitely spend some time volunteering—it gives you exposure and experience, and it lets programs know that you're serious about your career goal.

NETWORK ADMINISTRATOR

NAME: Nick Mitchell   **AGE:** 20

JOB TITLE: Network administrator/server engineer

FIELD(S): Information technology/ education

EMPLOYER: Marin County Office of Education

DEGREE: AA from a private trade school

COST: $20,000

TRAINING: Twelve levels of Microsoft certification

COST: About $1,000 each

SALARY: Starting: $45,000–50,000; three to six years experience: $70,000–90,000

WHAT DO YOU DO?

Technical support for the Marin County Office of Education and its employees. I'm loaned to other districts on a contract basis.

ACTIVITIES

Anything required to set up, repair, or maintain technical equipment. I set up voice mail systems, phone systems, and servers, repair copiers, develop networks—anything that the end user needs.

WHAT DO YOU LIKE ABOUT YOUR JOB?

Interacting with people and constantly adding to my knowledge base. There is always more to learn. I learn something new every day.

WHAT DON'T YOU LIKE ABOUT YOUR JOB?

I see people at a hard point of their day. Something doesn't work and they need if fixed right away.

HOW LONG HAVE YOU BEEN IN THIS JOB?

A year and a half. I'm also starting my own technical support business. I want to broaden my experience, make a bit of money, and sharpen my people skills.

WHAT IS YOUR ULTIMATE CAREER GOAL?

I'd like to be a college professor. Perhaps work at the school where I studied.

WHAT DO YOU SEE HAPPENING IN THIS FIELD IN THE NEXT FIVE TO TEN YEARS?

The field is becoming harder to get into. I have a friend from school who didn't do the Microsoft certifications. He isn't working.

NICK'S ADDITIONAL COMMENTS:

I love to learn. I'd be in school my whole life if it paid.

The impression that high schools give out, that you have to go to college to get a good job, is just wrong. If someone has an interest in a certain field, they should look into trade schools. I checked out community colleges, but liked the schedule at my trade school better. Classes were every day, Monday through Friday, from 8 a.m. to 3 p.m., year-round. I thought this made better use of my time than a regular college schedule. Also, I'm dyslexic. The smaller classes at the trade school were better for me because I could get more one-on-one help.

If someone wants to get a job in information technology, they should do internships to get their foot in the door. Go the extra mile and do certifications for common programs. These are a big help in getting a job.

PROFILE

SALES REP AND MANAGER

NAME: Cam Sanders   **AGE:** 29

JOB TITLE: Assistant state sales manager

FIELD(S): Surf industry/retail sales/clothing

EMPLOYER: Rip Curl Australia

DEGREE: None

COST: None

TRAINING: A lot surf trips

COST: Negligible

SALARY: Starting: $90,000 AUS; three to six years experience: depends on role

WHAT DO YOU DO?

Primarily, I'm a sales representative servicing forty-seven accounts with different product categories, including surf wear, men's accessories, watches, wet suits, footwear, eyewear, and mountain wear. I also help manage a state sales team with eleven staff members. I manage the reps and am responsible for management, sales and marketing strategies, state-based human-resource issues and assisting my state manager with his major accounts.

ACTIVITIES

I show our customers (buyers for retail stores) through the range of products and secure their orders in a prompt manner.

My job also includes building sales, demonstrating all product categories, and working with a territory partner who manages the girls' range of products.

We also work closely with our retailers if styles are proving to be successful and, if necessary, place additional orders.

DO YOU SUPERVISE ANYONE?

Yes, five representatives and three staff (a receptionist, a stock service representative, and a senior sales assistant).

HOW LONG HAVE YOU BEEN IN THIS JOB?

Nine months.

HOW DID YOU GET INTO THIS WORK?

After eight years in the financial planning industry, I found myself questioning my job and what I wanted to do. I had fallen into the financial planning industry, saw an opportunity, and worked my way up. I didn't have a degree and felt that I really needed one to succeed in the field of finance. I took six months off to think. The time made me realize that I was interested in one of my passions: surfing.

You hear the cliché, "You have to love what you do, because you are going to be doing it a lot." When I saw an opportunity within the surf industry, I applied and got an interview. I didn't get that position, but I was invited to apply for another one, which I did get.

WHAT DO YOU LIKE ABOUT YOUR JOB?

I love the lifestyle that is the surfing industry. Some may think that it means I go surfing every day, but our company and the surf industry has had significant growth and is becoming ever more corporate every day. We have come a long way from a company that was founded in Torquay, at Bell's Beach by two surfing mates way back in 1969. The main surfing companies are now listed companies that sell stock to the public and I would think we will go this way in the next five years.

WHAT DON'T YOU LIKE ABOUT YOUR JOB?

I get frustrated by the fact that it isn't as structured as it could be. It needs to be more process driven and more corporate. I get frustrated by not knowing more about my job, as it's still very new to me. After eight years in finance, I knew what needed to be done, how to do it, and if I had questions, I knew where I could go to get answers.

WHAT ARE THE MAIN CHALLENGES IN THIS INDUSTRY?

Like most industries, competition from other companies is a challenge. The line between surf and mainstream fashion has become blurred. This is a good and bad thing, but it endorses our success.

WHAT DO YOU SEE HAPPENING IN THIS FIELD IN THE NEXT FIVE TO TEN YEARS?

Most privately owned business will become listed entities. Wholesalers will buy up distribution networks (retail stores) and sell direct.

WHAT IS YOUR ULTIMATE CAREER GOAL?

Be successful in balancing work, life, and play. To be satisfied with whatever I have and to be able to put my head on the pillow knowing I have a clear conscience about what I did and who I am each day.

OTHER INTERESTS

Travel, snowboarding, architecture.

CAM'S ADDITIONAL COMMENTS

I have reduced my salary by about 60 to 75 percent, but I'm the happiest I have been in my entire working career. The Rip Curl motto is "The Search . . . It's closer than you think."

Strangely enough, it's a good analogy for my career thus far. The search is based on finding and experiencing new things—to travel around the next point to see what the surf is like. Importantly, it *is* closer than you think. I didn't have to go half the way around the world to find what I was looking for; it was right in my own backyard.

The important thing is to keep asking questions and reflecting on the answers. Don't be pressured into something you haven't fully considered. Come to your own conclusion and then pursue it.

SOFTWARE ENGINEER

NAME: Anson Wong   **AGE:** 24

JOB TITLE: Software engineer

FIELD(S): Computer technology/defense industry

EMPLOYER: Northrop Grumman Corporation

DEGREE: BS in computer science

COST: Approximately $45,000

STUDENT LOANS: $20,000

SALARY: Starting: $45,000: three to six years experience: $49,000–65,000

WHAT DO YOU DO?

Software development for a defense contractor, Northrop Grumman Corporation. I'm working on lab simulation software.

ACTIVITIES

Develop, design, maintain, document, and test software.

WHAT DO YOU LIKE ABOUT YOUR JOB?

Flexible schedule with a half day on Friday, socializing with people, and learning new things at work.

WHAT DON'T YOU LIKE ABOUT YOUR JOB?

Lack of organization for documents because it makes things harder to work with. Keeping work out of my time off.

HOW LONG HAVE YOU BEEN IN THIS JOB?

Nine months.

WHAT IS YOUR ULTIMATE CAREER GOAL?

I'd like to go into management.

WHAT DO YOU SEE HAPPENING IN THIS FIELD IN THE NEXT FIVE TO TEN YEARS?

The software field is growing and still in demand.

HOBBIES OR INTEREST OUTSIDE WORK

Running, Bible study club, traveling.

ANSON'S ADDITIONAL COMMENTS

It's hard to get a job these days. If you can get an interview, you're already lucky. In the interview, do something different. Make yourself stand out from the rest of the people. If you don't have any experience, show your projects and explain what you did and let them know why they should hire you.

Learning doesn't end once you get out of school. You'll be amazed by how much more there is to learn. You need to continue to learn as much as you can while you're still young.

P R O F I L E

TATTOO EQUIPMENT SALES

NAME: Brent Klingelhoefer   AGE: 23

JOB TITLE: Salesperson of supplies and equipment/tech support of supplies and equipment/customer service for products

FIELD(S): Service, technical support

EMPLOYER: DMS Tattoo & Body Piercing Supply

DEGREE: AA

TRAINING: No formal training for this job

SALARY: Starting: $10–14/hour; three to six years experience: $20,000 a year (part time)

WHAT DO YOU DO?

Direct sales to my customers, repairs of equipment (tattoo machines, thermal fax, autoclave, and others), fabrication.

ACTIVITIES:

Attend trade shows, meet with customers to discuss their needs, customer service.

WHO ARE YOUR CUSTOMERS?

My territory is a big chunk of Southern California.

HOW LONG HAVE YOU HAD THIS JOB?

Four years.

HOW DID YOU GET INTO THIS WORK?

Through a friend who was a tattoo artist.

WHAT DO YOU LIKE ABOUT YOUR JOB?

Travel, hands-on learning, and the variety of tasks.

WHAT DON'T YOU LIKE ABOUT YOUR JOB?

Dealing with customers' expectations. I'm in the surprising position of being the businessman dealing with artists. Our points of view are often very different.

WHAT ARE THE MAIN CHALLENGES IN THIS INDUSTRY?

Industry size has ballooned during the current tattoo craze. It's due for a downsizing. Tattoos still have a negative social stigma. Tattoo artists themselves can hurt the industry because they don't have business training. Carpal tunnel syndrome is also a problem.

WHAT DO YOU SEE HAPPENING IN THIS FIELD IN THE NEXT FIVE TO TEN YEARS?

Oversaturation of tattoo shops, more regulation from local health departments, followed by closings.

WHAT IS YOUR ULTIMATE CAREER GOAL?

Complete my BA. I have two terms left. I'm hopeful that I have a job waiting in the retail side of industry sales. I would love to be a homeowner now.

INTERESTS OUTSIDE OF WORK

Scion car club, travel, tattoos

BRENT'S ADDITIONAL COMMENTS

I'm a kinesthetic learner. I have worker hands; they need to be busy. When I first started my job, I took apart a tattoo machine once, and haven't had a problem understanding them since. If someone had told me how to do it or had given me a list of instructions, it wouldn't have been as easy.

I've learned the difference between want and need. I think other young people should too. For example, I *want* a Porsche. I *need* a dependable car that has room for my equipment and supplies. Or, I *want* filet mignon. I *need* to eat well to maintain my health and energy.

TEACHER

NAME: Alisa Harvey   **AGE:** 28

JOB TITLE: Social studies teacher

FIELD(S): Education

EMPLOYER: Beaverton (OR) School District

DEGREE: MA in teaching

COST: $40,000 (one and a half years at private liberal arts college)

TRAINING: Student teaching

COST: No additional cost; it's part of the MA program

SALARY: Starting: $34,200; three to six years experience: $40,000+

WHAT DO YOU DO?

I teach twentieth-century history. I have five classes of advanced history and regular history. I plan lessons. I might plan as many as three or four activities for a ninety-minute class. I also lecture, play documentary films, or coordinate role-playing and other simulations, and correct inappropriate behavior. Teaching requires me to be organized, disciplined, and patient. There is a tremendous amount of paperwork and red tape. Managing my classroom means that I must express myself clearly, give explicit instructions, and be prepared to change course when the lesson doesn't go as I had planned. As a teacher, I must be comfortable with public speaking and challenging unruly behavior. I must also be ready to drop everything and help a distressed student.

When I'm not teaching, I grade papers, work on lesson plans, read assigned texts, design assessment activities, contact parents, and conference with students. Professional development (staff meetings, trainings, and department activities) take much of my time.

DO YOU SUPERVISE ANYONE?

190 students a year!

HOW LONG HAVE YOU BEEN IN THIS JOB?

Two years.

HOW DID YOU GET INTO THIS WORK?

I began volunteering at a local high school, coaching an after-school mock trials program. We met three times a week, and since it was an extracurricular activity, the students were very motivated and eager to learn. People had always told me that I'd make a good teacher, and I suppose I knew deep down that it was going to be my life's work, but I had to try it out first. I contacted several of my former teachers and asked them about their jobs. I had been a student for years, but I knew practically nothing about being a teacher! It was an eye-opening experience.

WHAT DO YOU LIKE ABOUT YOUR JOB?

The kids are wonderful! They always make me laugh and I learn as much from them as they learn from me. I also like pursuing my interest in social history. In this modern world of mechanized jobs, I'm pleased that teaching can be so rewarding. It offers the opportunity to be creative, to be passionate, and to make a difference in the world.

WHAT DON'T YOU LIKE ABOUT YOUR JOB?

Class size and being paid for only eight hours a day. I might have as many as forty students, but I have been lucky to have classes as small as twenty-two. On the weekends, I often spend six to eight hours preparing for the week ahead. During a typical week, I work sixty to seventy hours.

WHAT ARE THE MAIN CHALLENGES IN THIS INDUSTRY?

Swelling class sizes are a tremendous concern. I cannot provide a truly adequate education for each and every student of mine when I manage a class load of 190 students. I simply cannot give them the one-on-one attention that they deserve. Low teacher pay is always an issue, and due to district budget cuts, jobs are not always secure.

WHAT DO YOU SEE HAPPENING IN THIS FIELD IN THE NEXT FIVE TO TEN YEARS?

Many schools are moving toward a small-school model. That means breaking large high schools of fifteen hundred plus students into three or four neighborhood or small schools. It's something I'd like to learn more about.

WHAT IS YOUR ULTIMATE CAREER GOAL?

To continue revising and improving my units of instruction. Ultimately, I would like to teach some additional subjects and possibly introduce some new courses.

OUTSIDE YOUR JOB, WHAT ARE YOUR OTHER INTERESTS OR HOBBIES?

I like to read historical fiction. Cooking is not my best skill, but I love to eat and spend time around a kitchen. When the weather is warm, I can be found in the garden planting flowers. Calligraphy is a hobby and traveling is a true passion.

ALISA'S ADDITIONAL COMMENTS

I've been told that teaching requires you to be a parent, counselor, friend, comedienne, disciplinarian, mentor, and actor. I certainly find that to be true! Teaching is not for everyone, but in spite of that, I'm always amazed to see how different types of people thrive in the classroom. Think of your favorite teachers—chances are they go about their jobs in a different way. Everyone who goes into teaching (and stays in the profession) must love working with people. It's a customer-service type of job.

For information about becoming a teacher, check this site: **www.pbs.org/firstyear/**

Index

NOTE: Page numbers followed by a *g* indicate a graph
Page numbers that are italicized indicate an illustration

About the Authors

RICHARD NELSON BOLLES has been a leader and the #1 celebrity in the career development field for more than thirty years. He was trained in chemical engineering at M.I.T.; in physics at Harvard University, where he graduated cum laude; and in New Testament studies at the General Theological (Episcopal) Seminary in New York City, where he earned a master's degree. He is the recipient of two honorary doctorates, is a member of MENSA, and is listed in *Who's Who in America* and *Who's Who in the World.* He lives in the San Francisco Bay Area with his wife Marci and one of his four children.

A career strategist since 1979, **CAROL CHRISTEN** has provided life/work planning and job search skill training to individuals and groups, specializing in working with teenagers using the internationally renown techniques found in *What Color Is Y Parachute?* She lives with her husband on a small farm on California's Central C where they raise colorful flowers and colorful chickens that lay lots of colorful

JEAN M. BLOMQUIST is a freelance editor and writer with experience as admissions counselor.

Also available from the Parachute Library

8.5 million copies sold

6 x 9 inches
432 pages

500,000 copies sold
Revised and expanded!

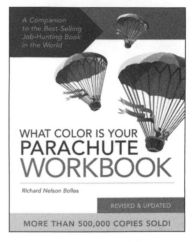

$8^{1/2}$ x 11 inches
48 pages